THE REASON I

Rise

LATOYA SHOCKENCY

ISBN 978-1-0980-9761-5 (paperback)
ISBN 978-1-0980-9762-2 (digital)

Christian Faith Publishing, Inc.
832 Park Avenue
Meadville, PA 16335
www.christianfaithpublishing.com

Printed in the United States of America

Welcome, everyone! I pray all is well, blessed, and you are living life to the fullest. This is just a short introduction to kind of let you know what you're about to read. It's all good as you read. You may read something and be like "Huh?" But keep reading. As I write it, I will break it down. Enjoy, be patient, and trust God!

I found what I would call my bestie, somebody I can talk to. He loves the Lord. He balances me and loves me. It's difficult, but not really because this is my testimony! Before I go any further, let me say this: this is my story. I hope you wouldn't judge me, but if you do, then so be it. God already knows what's going on with me. I know that what I'm about to say is going to help somebody. I don't want to make this about the relationship I have with God.

I want you to know how God is working for me. People seem to think you have to be a certain way in order to be loved by God, and that's not the case. God is genuine love. I'm not telling you to go out there and act the fool. What I am saying is use wisdom and do what you know is right. Just because someone doesn't agree with you and the decisions you make doesn't mean they're right.

Did you know that you and I, the people of God, make up the body of Christ? It's not just people who go to church. It's all of us. We are all God's children. We were all born into sin. Everybody's different. It took you a while before your life changed, and it's going to take the next person however long it takes for them to change, but don't give up on them. Now if you don't want anything out of life and you're doing wrong, that's between you and God, but God still loves you and can change anyone. We don't know the kind of life a person had or what they saw or had been through for a person to act the way they act. Our job is to pray for them and help them wherever God may allow.

2

For many years, I had it wrong. I was shy. I was listening to other people about my life and not trusting God to know what he was saying to me about my own life. People mean well, but I started to hear from God on my own, and my life started to change. And to tell you the truth, when my friend came into my life, that's when I started to see the bigger plan God had for my life. God was using him; and I needed to open my own eyes, ears, and mind and listen to what God was saying.

Do you think that a person can't be appointed by God because they drink occasionally or smoke? I don't know what your answer is, but God can use whoever he wants to. When I used to drink and smoke, God still kept me, loved me, and used me.

My friend is still dealing with some things, and we all are, but he loves God and God uses him. He's smart and has a gift from God and has favor with God. I'm not trying to get approval from you or say if this is right or wrong because I am my own person, and God leads the way for me. Some people think they're so holy that nobody should drink or smoke because they don't and they forget it took some time to get to that. It is really good people in the world that God uses or wants to use but some people won't talk to them because they don't think they're right.

Well, I feel like this: if you're right, why won't you help them without judging so that one day, they might put the drink down? I had to get that. God is about love and he's for all of us. God already

7

knows what you are doing and how it's going to turn out. Gods want to see us do the right thing in life and help his people. I believe in repentance, and God can change anybody because he's God. Through experience, I learned it takes time, and as long as you are seeking the Lord every day and praying to him, he's here for you and me.

I'm not a preacher or a minister. I don't know all the verses in the Bible, but I read the Bible, and wherever the Lord takes me in the Bible, I learn from it. What I'm saying is my calling isn't to preach. We all have different callings, some the same, some different. I don't know what it takes to be a preacher because God didn't give me that. What I want to be is whatever God wants for my life and what I love to do is help any way I can.

I have overcome a lot of pain and struggles. From this day forward, I will be a blessing for people. I learned you have to use wisdom the Lord gave you. If not, you could be taken for granted, and I got tired of going through this with family friends and relationships. I wanted to know how to stop getting hurt and how to treat a person so that if I say something, they won't get hurt or offended. That was really important to me, and again, God used my friend to help me with that.

It'll probably be a lot of talk about my friend because when he came into my life, that's when I picked up on some things that I thought I had mastered, but a lot had to be adjusted and situated. Now I'm better in my spirit. I have one of the best pastors ever you would have to visit The Forever Living Church of God. To know what I'm talking about, my pastor has been here for me for years, and I thank God for her. Truly, as I write, I just want to encourage somebody that might be feeling like you're so bad to keep your head up and believe you're good and stand on that. God's got you. Don't let it bother you when somebody says you still do this or you still do that. Say, "Yes, I do, but God knows what I do. It's personal with me and Jesus, and he's bringing me through. I took myself through too much and I refuse to go back, so prayerfully, you can love me for who I am because this is me."

I will listen to anybody, and I love advice. The final decision will be God's. I pray we stop judging and hating each other. I believe after you finish reading this book, someone is gonna feel like they needed to hear this.

4

I have two sons by two different daddies. They turned out to be good kids. I'm proud of them for staying focused. Both Kyland and Kevin are juniors. They are seven years apart, and both of them have seen a lot growing up, but they know without God, life would have been completely different. They are a lot like me. They have good dads that were brought up right and haven't forgotten where they came from.

I was not married when I had them, and the Lord didn't punish me for that. Thank you, Jesus. I'm not saying purposely have kids and don't be married. I'm just saying you never know how life will turn out. Keep the faith and live it. The Bible is right. Everything in it I refuse to walk through life without God.

A lot of times, we are too hard on ourselves, and that's what the devil wants. God has the whole plan for our life. Sometimes, we take a detour, but I believe if we know some of these things I'm saying, our experience with God would be a lot easier.

People try to scare you, but God has taught me to take it slow and humble myself because he's in charge, and that's what I live by. If you know you're a good person, hold onto that. Don't let anything take it away from you. God will start to show you things. Do your best to be the best person you know how. That's what God wants to see. He'll do the rest. Believe you are good, and do good. Watch what the Lord's going to do for you.

5

How are you feeling today? Are you doing well? I pray that you are. Have you been worrying way too much about things you have no control over? Don't hold on to that. Let it go. It's just another trick from the devil, trying to keep you confused so he can tear you apart. This is why I wanted to write this book because people need to know the devil's tricks and how he doesn't want us to get ahead in life. Pay attention to your surroundings so you don't get tricked by the enemy. Have an ear for God. We should know his voice. He is all love and positive. If it doesn't sound like that, it's not God.

Don't listen to that devil. Say, "You a lie and I rebuke you in the name of Jesus!" And move on also. Don't sit idle.

Pastor Stewart taught me that by getting busy doing God's will, God will give you the rest you need when you need it. It's not hard as we make it. The experiences I had throughout life up until now made me feel like it's been rough, but forget about that. Pick yourself up. You have gifts and talents inside you that can help someone, but if you always are down on yourself or doubting yourself, we won't be able to see the pureness in you, and that's what God wants to see: the peace of God in you so he can bring it out. It's about God helping you so he can bless you to help the next person.

God gave us Jesus as an example to help us on earth. God knew we would make mistakes. Correction is good. Look at it this way: if you do something wrong or get it messed up, don't leave it like that.

Ask God for help till you get it right. Read the directions. Start over. That's what Jesus came to do, help us till we are fixed. And even after, there's more work to be done. He does not leave us half done. God is amazing. We can get this right.

Can I share something with y'all? We must love everybody. No one is exempt from love. We have to get that for our good.

I have to tell you, even people that treat you bad, talk about you, lie to you, all that stuff—yes, you have to love them too.

Wait a minute, I'm not suggesting you be a fool for people, but I had to learn, and it was a process that in order for me to be truly happy in my spirit, I would have to love people unconditionally with the love of God. I know you're saying, "Well, what about the ones that mistreated me, and I know I didn't deserve it?"

Well, yes, them too. You may have to hold your peace or bite your tongue, but it'll be all right. What doesn't kill you makes you stronger. The way I feel, I never felt like this ever. It's hard to believe it, but I appreciate it because it's not me. The glory is the Lord's. I'm his vessel, and I thank God. He made room for my life.

All my life, I had to fight. Lol. Naw, I'm just kidding. That's off the movie *The Color Purple*. Oprah Winfrey said that.

Seriously, don't give up on people, and don't give up on yourself. Every day you wake up, get up, ready to start your day by thanking God for waking you up and for bringing you through the night. Ask God to help you and be with you as you move around, doing things. Ask God to give you clear sound so you can hear his voice and thank him for doing it. We have everything to be thankful for.

My pastor always says, "Thank him for tying your shoes." She says, "I love you, Lord." That's a prayer for eighteen, almost twenty years. I went through hell, but it's okay because guess what? As I was going through the fire, God was in me. He held me up when I wanted to break. He covered me when I couldn't do it for myself, and as messed up as I was, God still loved me. It's a must that I share what God has given me.

Keep living a life to please God. It's going to get better and better. God is in control. God is who I answer to. Don't get upset about that. If I'm not right or if I'm doing something wrong, the Lord will let me know. God doesn't need us to tear each other down. We're supposed to love each other, no matter what, and that's what I plan to do.

7

*I*f God says no, then it's no. Not man or woman; it's important to know who is speaking to you, meaning the Lord or the enemy. When God speaks to me, I may ask or pray for something, and immediately I'll know if it's okay with God because if things get to feeling off in my spirit, then I know God doesn't want me to do that. Or if I say something that's not right, immediately God will correct me.

When you get corrected, don't get upset. God doesn't want you to be confused or not know what you're talking about, so in correction, he makes it clear he'll start to reveal himself to you and show you things you always wanted to know. Keep God in your life. It's a better way, totally, and I'm saying that as humble as I know how because it's something to shout about.

But that's another thing I learned. God doesn't require us to holler and scream when we're praising him. I used to think that was what it was all about. I'm not saying you won't make a joyful noise until the Lord because when it hits you, it hits you. I look at it this way: If I'm hollering and screaming, I can't hear God. To me, it's just like if I was in an argument and it's too loud, but when I humble myself and pray and thank God, I hear him clearly.

8

Would you rather know the truth or a lie? I learned with God that we have to be examples. If I can't help you, then I'd rather not say anything, and I hope you would do the same for me. We all have a job here on earth for the Lord. Be your best in everything you do. Every day, do something to encourage somebody. Say something nice. Give a loan, anything that can make somebody's day. Treat me the way I treat you. That's fair what they say. Even exchange ain't no robbery. I can deal with that, and God says whatever measure you use to judge, the same will be measured to you, so we have to be careful how we treat people. Our flesh always wants to rise up, but the devil is a liar. He can't have me. Not this time, Satan, and no other time. Kill the flesh and rise above.

9

*J*used to hurt when I couldn't find one person to love me like God does. It took me a long time to understand that, and the devil had me mad about it. As I kept living, stuff kept happening as I went through it. I started to understand there's only one Lord, and if people aren't making me feel like I wanted to feel, I was expecting too much out of them. That's not their job. You get that kind of love from God. Then you can give some love and won't expect too much from a person.

You can drain people, and it's not right. God has everything we need. Life has enough for us to do than to be needy and clingy to a person. It's not fair, I understand, if you need help or advice but don't do too much if we calm down and listen. My friend says that all the time. It's not as big a deal as we make it.

10

*E*verybody's not gonna be the same. I'm glad we're all different in our own way. God made everything we see, even you and me. He did it so nicely, everything in order, no mess-ups—perfect. Thank you, Holy Father!

When God made us, he put something special in all of us, and as we grow to know God, he allows us to give it out. It's better to give than to receive as you give it out. God is putting it in. We will never be empty with God.

*T*his page is dedicated to my pastor, Pastor Mattie Stewart. I said it before, and I'm going to say it again. I thank you, Jesus Christ, for a wonderful woman of God. Oh my God. I wanna say this right. She has instilled so much in me through the relationship she has with God. It is awesome to see how God moves in her life, and it's a gift from God to know her.

Her walk with God is so plain to see. She does it really well. She has a sweet loving spirit. She's humble and a beautiful person. She calls me her spiritual daughter. I believe I've been knowing Pastor Stewart for over almost seventeen years now. She has seen me go through some serious stuff. I know she could see how messed up I really was, but she never told me.

Over the years, I learned that Pastor Stewart could see people and knew who I was, but with the love she has for God, she only wanted to see my life changed, and I appreciate her for that. It's a blessing to look back over my life and see how she encouraged me, even though she knew the things she knew. If God's grading on pastoral duties, I know for sure she's passing with flying colors. I dedicate a special place in my heart for you, Pastor. To God be the glory! Thank you for being who you are in Christ and for doing what you do. Love you!

12

*W*ill I ever get married again? I surely will. I see marriage as a partnership. You should always be able to talk to your spouse, but if God is not in it, it won't last, and I believe that's with any relationship, friendship, and even family. Also, God has to be the head of whatever we do or the devil will come and destroy it, and it has to be both parties in agreement.

The Bible says, how can two walk together except they agree? That is such a true statement. If you believe in one thing and your partner believes something else, that's not walking together. You can have your own opinion about things, but at the end of the day, we should have talked and worked things out so that we're on the same page.

Learn to get an understanding. It's not about who's right or wrong. It's about coming together as one, making the marriage work. Men, you're supposed to love your wives like Christ loves the church. And women are supposed to submit to our husbands as long as he is following Christ. Marriage is a lovely gift from God. If we can get it right with our spouse, it will be unbreakable.

*B*e careful what you put in your spirit. Don't get me wrong, there's a reason for everything. Don't shoot anybody down for what they say. The Lord will give you what to say if you're patient with him. Sometimes you have to be still. The Holy Spirit is the greatest gift we could ever receive. That is the reason any chance I get, I'm going to give back what God has given me.

God blesses us with the Holy Spirit freely. What we must do is allow God in our hearts, repent, and let God live in us. Remember, no weapon formed against me shall prosper, so don't be afraid to get out there and do God's will. If he's in you, then he's got you.

*P*lease don't be a disturbance to the Holy Spirit. God is doing great things. He will have his way. There's a time to listen, and there's a time to speak!

ABOUT THE AUTHOR

Toya Shockency is a very outgoing person. She loves to write books, poems, music, etc. She loves the Lord with all her heart. Toya says she is not perfect, but she is striving for perfection.

Toya is a mother of two, and both her boys have other siblings from their dads. In the daytime, Toya teaches children. She is forty-three years old and proud of her age. Some people are ashamed of their age.

Toya loves family, shopping, and singing—she really just likes to have a good time. She keeps it real and loves honesty, and if you ask her opinion, she's going to tell you the truth to best help you.

Toya has two sisters and one brother. Both her parents are in her life. God is awesome. Life is good. God bless.

I pray my book is going to inspire someone who doesn't know the Lord or is struggling with their walk with Christ. It's really to let someone know it's all right, don't be so hard on yourself. God loves you no matter what. This book is to let people know not to forget where they come from. It's a blessing to be saved, but it takes a lifetime to get there.

I felt encouraged to write this book because I feel like there's a message, and people need to hear it enjoy and be blessed!

Christian Faith
PUBLISHING

$11.95

ISBN 978-1-0980-9761-5

51195

9 781098 097615

FOUND

Swiping right on me to *find love*

JULIE DEMSEY

A catalogue record for this book is available from the National Library of Australia

FOUND

Swiping right on me to find love

Julie Demsey

*To love, kindness
and a better world.*

Contents

Prologue

The only piece of furniture in my new home is an air mattress, and even that is borrowed. But at least I can breathe. I am free. Well ... physically free, but technically still married until we can come to a settlement. I'm emotionally free, too, and I couldn't be happier. At least, that's what I keep telling myself so I don't fall apart at the prospect of learning how to navigate life as a single person again. I never imagined I would be needing to do that. I'm not at all sure how to prepare myself.

I'm surprised I can't hear the echo of the pen hitting the paper as I write this. The only other possible sound would be me shifting on the air mattress. It feels really, really good to be in my very own home, even if that is all I own – the place itself. Strike that, I guess I don't even own that; the bank does. I do have clothes. At least I can get dressed and go to work tomorrow so I can continue to chip away at this new mortgage. But sitting here with my freshly painted empty walls, I feel like I can breathe. And in this moment that seems like a lot.

Even if it comes with a bit a fear and a lot of not wholly
welcomed vulnerability, there is a certain sense of comfort in
knowing I am free to do this on my own terms - I just need to
figure out what those are. Because, if I am really honest, I have
no idea what my terms are or how to figure out what they
should be or could be.

MY UNCLE SERVED ME MY FIRST BEER AND TAUGHT ME HOW TO HAVE
cocktail hour as I was sitting in the sandbox at age four. Clearly, he
started teaching me life skills early on. So when I called to tell him
about the demise of my marriage and he replied, "You know, Julie,
there's a reason divorce is so expensive; it's worth it. Just give it some
time, you will see," I figured he was right. I came to learn that expense
wasn't just financial – it was mental as well. It took some time to get
my finances back in order, but it took just as much time to get my mind
back in order, too, and rediscover who I had been *before* my seven-year
marriage – and, more importantly, who I actually was in general and
whether that was who I wanted to be. While I definitely lost a part of
myself in the marriage, it's probably more apt to say I entered into the
marriage because I was already lost. I just hadn't realized I'd spent so
much time looking for the approval of those around me that I'd led
myself into a relationship I'd believed I should want.

This started as my tale of getting back into single life and exploring
online dating, and turned into a journey of looking for love and finding
myself. Writing this has allowed me to heal, to learn (probably more
than I bargained for) and to get closer to *finding myself* and becoming
the woman *I choose* to be.

I'm no different than you. I could be the girl next door, just trying to figure out life after divorce and navigate the world of dating – online dating in particular, since that seems to be the only way we meet these days. I had no idea what I was in store for or what I was about to learn. As a transformational mindset coach and hypnotherapist, it's not lost on me that it took a lot of time and effort to come face to face with my own fears and limiting beliefs around myself, sex and relationships. If only I was able to help myself as quickly and competently as I've been able to help my clients! The thing is, we can be really book smart, but we aren't actually taught these love and life things, so we have to figure them out on our own. They *should* be taught! We need this help and insight, and that's why I love the work I do now. I get to help the younger generation learn some of these lessons early on and build their sense of self. I get to guide older generations through smashing their limiting beliefs and updating their connection to themselves and others. But then, I think we are all on our own journey in these things. I do wish I knew then what I know now, and I am grateful for the skills and insights I picked up later in life, especially as I started my coaching and hypnotherapy practice.

I've shared these stories with you in the hope you find them relatable in a way that brings some comfort and solace, and a few laughs too. Remember, you are not alone; we all experience uncertainties in navigating the world of dating and relationships and finding our true selves.

xo, Julie

P.S. There are no actual names in the book other than mine. This is intentional, of course, to protect the innocent and not-so-innocent participants. Besides, this is *my* story, not theirs. The cast of characters in this book could have a very different point of view on what happened … or not. I know I have certainly seen things differently over time. Locations and names of places were also left out intentionally because, really, these experiences could happen to anyone almost anywhere, even to *you* if you let them.

CHAPTER ONE

Back to the beginning

WHY IS IT THAT WHEN GIRLS START LIKING BOYS, WHEN A BOY doesn't like them back they ask themselves, "What's wrong with me? Why doesn't he like me?" instead of "What's wrong with him that he doesn't like an amazing girl like me?" I don't think anyone ever instructed me to think it was me rather than them; for some reason that thinking came naturally. But why? And why did it never occur to me to question those thoughts? Was it deeply engrained in my DNA? Passed through generations? Or just so regularly portrayed in media and advertising that it seemed the only plausible reality? Whatever the answer, it certainly colored my teenage years and sadly, I imagine, those of too many other girls on the planet. "Am I not …

pretty

skinny

popular

fun

smart enough?"

And the list goes on …

If only those thoughts ended in the teenage years, but no. In my case, at least, they stayed with me for decades.

My sexual repression

I was nine or ten when I had my first crush on a boy. We had a school fair and I made sure to be next to him on the cake walk (think musical chairs with the last one standing getting a cake as a prize). For everyone else, the point of the game was to be the last one standing on a block and win the cake … But for me, the prize was to be close to this boy and have him notice me. I was so focused on him and worried about whether he liked me that I ended up embarrassing myself by walking off when he got called out, even though I was still in the game. The teacher kept calling to me to come back to my place. It seems like a small thing but the heat from my cheeks burned deeply into my soul and I kept playing over the embarrassment in my mind for weeks on end, sure that now no boy would ever like me.

Fast forward to junior high, high school, college and even further, and my thoughts were all still the same. I would set my sights on a boy (and later a man) I had a crush on and think of all the reasons he would never like me and how lucky I would be if, for some reason, he decided he did. Retrospectively, I can see that even though I felt so at the time, I wasn't the unpopular ugly duckling no boy would ever like – I had my fair share of boys who *did* like me, but I never felt or believed I was worthy or that it was actually possible. I would worry they were playing a terrible joke, pretending to like me so they could make fun of me, or using me for some reason or another. It sounds so silly to me now, but I spent day after day and night after night, way too much time over a lifetime, with my head filled with those thoughts, trying hard to be or become the girl and then the woman they would like and love. I never gave a thought or consideration to whether that would be a person *I* would like to be. That didn't ever occur to me.

My thinking about sex was just as clouded. *Even if a boy acts like he loves me or tells me he loves me, he is just doing that to get sex. And if I give in and have sex with him, he is likely to dump me the next day.* I never, ever considered if I actually *wanted* to have sex or if I felt any sexual desire. That did not come into the equation *at all.* Why was that? How did it never even cross my mind to consider my own wants and desires? Probably because the only want and desire I could fathom was to be liked and loved. I didn't have any wants or desires of my own, other than thinking things like, *How lucky am I to be a freshman making out with this popular senior boy? I guess it feels kind of nice. I want him to like me, so I am not going to tell him he has to stop trying to unbutton my jeans because if I say that, he won't like me. So, instead, I'll just kind of wiggle away and then redo the button while we are making out and he'll keep liking me.*

When my mother asked how in the world I could have broken the button off my jeans, I simply shrugged my shoulders and ignored her like a typical teenager. I couldn't tell her the truth: I was just doing what I thought I needed to do to get a boy to like me.

How did I come up with these ridiculous sensibilities and beliefs? Did my mother constantly tell me I needed to protect my virtue when I was in utero, thinking maybe the message would seep into my subconscious and stop me from divesting myself of my virginity at too early an age? Or did I get these thoughts and ideas from all the novels I read as a young girl, or all the movies I watched? Was I so programmed to be a good girl who did as she was told that I wasn't capable of developing my own thoughts, desires and beliefs? Was this so deep-seated that for decades it never crossed my mind to consider my own wants and desires? How and where did I learn, or come to think it was more important, to please others and get them to like me? I'm guessing it was a strong dose of nature and nurture combined. I look back now and it saddens me deeply that I spent so many years thinking this way.

ℊ

ALL THROUGH HIGH SCHOOL, I NEVER CONSIDERED EITHER 'GOING all the way' or saying out loud to a boy to **stop** because if I did either, I was sure I would get dumped. I didn't want that to happen. I wanted more than anything for them to like me. Somehow that seemed more important than *me* liking me. I was a straight A student – how could I be so smart and at the same time have so little confidence and consideration for myself?

The funny thing (not actually funny, more sad) is that I ended up getting dumped anyway for *not* having sex. My first boyfriend in high school, the love of my life, my everything (perhaps this was more my teenage perception than the reality) actually dumped me because I *wouldn't* have sex with him. So how well did holding onto that prized virginity work for me? As much as I *loved* him, I certainly wasn't mentally ready to have sex. I didn't really know what to do and was a bit intimidated by the whole idea. A good make-out session was nice, but when he kept trying to push my head down, I had no concept of what he was doing. When he finally explained, I was mortified and disgusted. I couldn't figure out why he would want me to put *that* in my mouth. I must have been absent the day they talked about oral sex in sex education class!

I was only 14. Was I supposed to be mentally and physically ready for more? I certainly didn't know enough to consider that question, and I didn't feel sexual desire because I had been adequately brainwashed into thinking I, as a female, shouldn't have sexual desire. That was something only the males and the bad girls had. Sadly, some of those thoughts and beliefs didn't end with high school – they stuck with me for decades to come.

Losing my V-card

I never thought about having my *first sexual encounter*, I thought about *losing my virginity*. And those thoughts were filled with fears of being used and discarded rather than happy visions of romance and enjoying an experience with someone I cared deeply about. Was I the only outlier who felt that way or were other girls feeling the same? And why didn't I question at the time why a girl was seen as *losing* her virginity or *giving it* up, while a boy was seen as *taking* virginity and *becoming* a man? I bought into the notion that my virginity was something that would be taken or lost, rather than coming to the conclusion that I deserved to be a sexual being and derive pleasure from the experience. Why didn't I know this was something I should enjoy doing with someone else, not something I should have done to me?

ℒ

I *FINALLY* LOST MY VIRGINITY THE SUMMER AFTER MY FIRST YEAR OF college at the age of 17. After years spent worrying about whether a guy was going to like me and making sure I was the type of woman he would like, I layered on the worry that I had now become too old to be a virgin. Add into the stew of thoughts floating around my head the new stress of worrying that the longer I waited, the more anxious I would be about having sex with someone so much more experienced than I was, coupled with beginning to worry about if I would find someone who would want to marry me one day ... and I have to wonder how I had any room in my head to study and get good grades.

When I finally had sex for the first time, the encounter happened solely because I decided it was time to *lose my virginity*, not because I was in love or lust or even like, nor because I was busting with desire.

At that point, if I had any desire other than to find someone to love me, that sexual desire was still so deeply repressed I couldn't in any way, shape or form imagine acknowledging it. I was too busy following orders, doing what I was told to in life and trying to fit in and be liked – my mind never seemed to know it could wander into the territory of thinking about what I liked and wanted, let alone venture to the land of desire.

It was summer break after my first year of college and the last time I lived back with my parents. I had a summer job but was still fairly carefree and, as a college student on summer break is, I was more concerned with enjoying my time off before I headed back to school than anything else.

At that point, perhaps I should have been wondering why a 31-year-old man wasn't bothered to learn the woman he was dating wasn't in fact twenty-something but was actually only 17. Or why, as a carefree 17-year-old, I was dating him in the first place? Was it a desire to be more grown up? More likely it was because he took me to concerts and fancy restaurants with nice wine. And he liked me! If someone so much older and put together liked me, I must be a good person, right?

One night it happened. We were at his (very adult, nothing college dorm about it) place having a glass of wine at the end of the evening. He started kissing me and then, very seriously, said, "I want to make love with you." I am not sure which struck first: sheer panic or the repulsion at his terminology. I've never been able to get the words 'making love' to form in or exit my mouth, and it was worse when I heard someone else saying the words 'make love' or 'let's make love'. It gets even worse when those little words are aimed at me. Even to this day, any sense of desire I may have been feeling vanishes. It's the female equivalent of losing my erection, and then some.

And if that wasn't enough of a cold bucket of ice being dumped over me, my thoughts replaced any crumb of desire with fear: *How do I handle this? What do I do? I feel at this age I should lose my virginity, but I am completely terrified by the idea of looking like an idiot, not knowing what to do or how to do it ... he's 31; surely he must understand he has a lot more experience than I do and this is going to freak me out.*

I am sure it didn't cross his mind I was a virgin. He certainly wasn't speaking to me or treating me like the inexperienced woman I actually was, and I certainly wasn't prepared to have that discussion or get naked with him. I started to feel shy and a bit sick to my stomach at the same time ... so much so, I seem to have wiped from my memory what I said and how I gracefully, or perhaps not so gracefully, worked my way out of the situation at that moment.

Did I say I was starting to feel allergic to his cat that had been circling us, or simply it was getting to be past my curfew? Either response seems like it could have been plausible. I only know one thing for sure; I was not about to have my first sexual experience with a man who likely had a decade and change more experience than I had in the sheets. I didn't actually say what I was thinking, which was, *Hold that thought please, I need to go get rid of my virginity with someone closer to my age so I am not intimidated and embarrassed by my lack of experience, and then I'll be back,* but I put that plan in motion the following day.

In my fucked-up, scared, virgin mind, the only plausible solution to this problem was to first have sex with someone more experienced than me, but with not as much experience as him. Yes, a smarter solution might have been to have a conversation with him about the fact I was a virgin and nervous. But no, that solution didn't even cross my mind – if I let him know any of that, he might not like me anymore. In my 17-year-old mind, it seemed much more plausible to go find an ex-boyfriend who was just a couple of years older than me and finally *give in*, give him what he had always wanted and have sex with him.

The plan worked like a charm. The old boyfriend was ready and willing to deflower me and so, being the good little problem solver I was, I made that happen. It certainly wasn't anything soft, sensual and caring. What I actually got was a 21-year-old guy who, while rumored to have lots of experience, had no finesse whatsoever. It felt like he was trying to push and then rapidly pound a square peg into a round hole. Nothing pleasurable or enjoyable about it. After what was likely a few minutes, but felt like eons, it stopped. We were apparently done, or at least he was, and I lay there overly aware of my nakedness and disappointment, thinking … *That's it? Ugh. That was not in any way close to earth-shattering, but it got the deed done. Operation relinquish virginity accomplished.* It was just a simple tick off my to-do list and I didn't have to worry about being dumped, because I wasn't in love and I had no desire to have sex with this guy again.

I was ignorant to the idea that this way of losing my virginity was a stupid way of protecting my heart that ended up robbing me of what could have been a much better experience and a fond memory. And I never did end up *making love* with the older guy either. After that experience, the idea of him somehow became less appealing and I backed away from the relationship with him, knowing I would soon be leaving to go back to college anyhow. At the time, I didn't understand what I had done to myself or why I had done it; I was just relieved the whole situation got me to take action against ending up the last virgin alive! Unfortunately, it didn't lead me on a quest to start considering my own desire.

From dating to divorce

Looking back over my dating history, I certainly had my fair share of dates, had some longer-lasting relationships and broke quite a few hearts for someone who never thought herself attractive enough or skinny enough or interesting enough for anyone to ever want her. I feel sadness now that it took me until after my divorce (and into my fourth decade on this planet) to think about myself as a sexual being and really enjoy sex for what it is rather than getting caught up and worrying only about the unspoken power dynamics behind it.

That's not to say I didn't have fun or get into relationships I enjoyed, but I was never completely free and relaxed about sex because I was always worried about what it *meant* instead of enjoying how it felt. Filling my mind were so many negative thoughts and concerns about how soon I should have sex with someone I was dating, and then if how often we were doing it was often or not often enough, and what that meant and would that actually lead to the right type of relationship? Would that get someone to marry me or betray me? These thoughts weren't *always* at the forefront of my mind, but they were always at the back of my mind along with, 'Does he like me?', 'Where is this relationship going?' and 'Will he dump me?'

For someone who was a natural optimist about most things, I was overly pessimistic and negative about *my* place in relationships. If only I could go back and tell the younger me those were the wrong thoughts and questions. The thoughts should have been that I was amazing and worthy and deserving, and I should have been asking, 'Do I like him and how I feel when I am with him?', 'Am I having fun with him and are we satisfying each other in and out of bed?' and 'Does he treat me well and do I treat him well in return?' If only I had been wise enough to have that in mind earlier in life …

ᡃ

WHILE I DIDN'T HAVE THOSE QUESTIONS FORMULATED WHEN I WAS in my mid-thirties and met my ex-husband, I *thought* I knew enough and had enough experience to know for sure he was *The One* and our relationship was the real deal. When we went out on dates, time would fly by as we talked and talked, often sharing a last glass of wine after dinner as a restaurant shut down around us. In my mind, we were completely open with each other and shared all the right things. I never worried about if he would call, or if I should wait for him to call; somehow one of us always contacted each other at the right time and it was just *easy*.

Before I knew it, we were making plans further out into the future than the length of time we had known each other and to far away locations and family gatherings. I never worried about where the relationship was going because I just knew and trusted we would continue to be together. It felt right. I'd never been in a relationship that was *so easy*, so when six months in we went away for the weekend and he surprised me with a proposal, I didn't hesitate to say YES! I was finally getting what I had always wanted, right? A man who loved me and wanted to marry me. Another tick off my to-do list in the next step of properly adulting, or so I naively thought.

Once we were engaged, everything somehow became difficult. I didn't understand. Everything was an argument. I couldn't do anything right. That sweet, loving, gentle man became angry and began treating me like I was the enemy instead of his biggest champion. At first,

I thought it was the stress of planning the wedding, and then I continued to tie it to the stress of one thing or another. I always made an excuse because I remembered the beautiful times and how lovely he could be. Besides, I had done everything I was supposed to do ... I'd landed a man who wanted to marry me, so things couldn't be that bad, could they? Even with the emotional rollercoaster leading up to it, we had a beautiful wedding, because that is what one does and I was the *ultimate doer*. When I was doing, I made sure I was doing things well.

We settled into married life with ups and downs and all-consuming jobs that allowed us to buy our first home. As we went on, that beautiful, easy relationship we had leading up to the engagement transformed into something that left me on edge, walking on eggshells. Of course, there were happy, loving times too, but more often than not it was a very mentally unhealthy situation. Not that I gave it much thought at the time; I just persevered. The memory of him at his best at the very beginning kept me going. That was the same man, wasn't it? And I had made a commitment. I was taught to honor and keep my commitments and to always finish what I started. Not seeing things through and giving them my all was failure. So I carried on as best I could, not knowing what to do to make the situation, my marriage and our lives better.

I hadn't yet noticed that in actioning what I had been taught, I was taking care of and pleasing others rather than ever remotely considering I deserved to figure myself and my wellbeing into the equation. In my mind, I didn't see behaving in that way as healthy – I had been taught that was selfish and self-centered and I didn't want to be those things.

I stuck to my commitment to that man and that marriage for seven years, hoping it was a phase and it could get better if I just tried a little harder. I kept trying until one day …

I

just

couldn't

try

anymore.

I was beaten down, dejected and tired … burnt out, really. I had allowed that to happen because I, with all my programming to date, believed the whole of the relationship and my commitment to it was more important than *me*. My glass, which was always half full, had been obliterated by his glass that was always half empty. I'd promised myself in a previous serious relationship that when the bad outweighed the good I would end things. I had that time, but this time I was married. So I tried more and I tried harder and after trying everything and every type of couples counseling we could without any positive progress, I finally came to know I had to leave if I wanted a chance at a happy, healthy life.

As hard as life was in that marriage, something inside my head kept signaling that the easier thing at the time would have been to stay. Because that was what I had been taught was the right thing to do. Because that was what I had been programmed to do – that was what was expected of me, and I had always followed the path I thought I was supposed to. In general, my way of being had been to not rock the boat, to keep everyone happy, even when someone was doing their best to capsize that boat with me in it. I'd just keep up the outward appearance that everything was fine, and just maybe it would be.

In the end, I finally woke up and chose to save myself; I finally chose *me*. I knew I had a lot of life ahead of me and chose that rather than sinking down into negativity and depression with him. I had to stop looking after him and start looking after myself. That was one of the hardest things I have ever done. It felt like I was breaking all the rules I had been given. It felt selfish and ungrateful and like I was giving up and failing. And that was what I was feeling even before I ended it. Telling him it was over, that it was time for us to part ways, was not easy, it was not pretty and it was terribly ugly and painful at times. The whole process was messy and awful – so much so, it nearly broke me. *He* nearly broke me. But I knew deep inside it was necessary for my survival and the only plausible way forward.

ℒ

I HAD THOUGHT THAT WAS MY FOREVER RELATIONSHIP. THOSE FIRST six magical months settled me into a false sense of security that we were headed towards decades of happiness. But I was wrong. I could blame him for undisclosed mental issues, but under those he was a beautiful man. I could just as easily blame myself for not being strong enough or confident enough at the time to stop him from allowing my light to dim or to stand up to him and the issues there were, rather than backing down when he made accusations about my intentions. But in the end, blame doesn't need to be placed – it doesn't help anything. We both did the best we could with the tools we had at the time.

CHAPTER TWO

Starting again

I READ *EAT, PRAY, LOVE* AND DIDN'T UNDERSTAND HOW IT WAS possible or why it was necessary to dissolve into a hysterical puddle on the bathroom floor at the end of a marriage. Maybe I was just afraid that if I started to cry, I would open up a deep, dark hole of despair I would never be able to crawl back out of. I was the stoic one, the unemotional workaholic robot, according to my family and many of my closest friends. I was, by all accounts, successful and shouldn't want for anything; crumbling shouldn't be on my agenda. If I just kept going, maybe the divorce would be only a hiccup in my privileged life.

I wasn't able to break down or show weakness or vulnerability. It simply wasn't in my nature because it wasn't expected of me or how others saw me. And if I *did* break, who would take care of me anyhow? I wasn't allowed that luxury. I was always so busy taking care of others I inadvertently banished my own needs, if I even considered having any. I was one of the fortunate ones, so it would be inappropriate to complain or call attention to my issues when others were far worse off. So I did what I always did and what I had been trained to do; I soldiered on, got a new, bigger job and bought a new home. I took every action that was expected of me on the preordained life path that felt like it had been chosen for me. I always did what was expected of me. The divorce was the first time I'd strayed.

So what was I to supposed to do now? No one had ever taught me what came next – I hadn't even considered that. I had only known something had to change before I no longer existed.

Taking time for me

I was so ignorant of my deeper emotions and the toll the marriage and divorce took on me, I figured I could just easily pick myself up and keep going. I did my best to ignore the signs something wasn't quite right. I'd be sitting in my now-furnished apartment, happy and at peace reading a book, and then, without warning, a feeling of anxiousness would course though my body, leaving me unsettled. I was jumpy and on edge. Even though I was by myself, that feeling I lived with for seven years didn't magically disappear – that *knowing* that the calm led to a storm and I needed to have my fight or flight response ready at all times. There was still no true relaxing. That hypervigilance, it would seem, didn't just disappear overnight along with the ex.

I was at least smart enough to realize this way of being probably wasn't normal, and rather than jumping right out and looking for another relationship, I needed some time to just be on my own, figure things out and begin to heal. Truth be told, I had absolutely no interest in spending time dating or getting into a new relationship at that point. How would I be able to trust myself not to make a mistake again and get into a relationship with the wrong person? I didn't know how to prepare myself for that.

Plus, the idea of one day needing to get out there and negotiate the world of dating wasn't sounding very appealing. Everything had changed since I was last single. And oh my, after almost a decade, at some point in time someone was going to see my body ... naked. That was such a different concern in my forties than it was in my thirties. I couldn't imagine being seen. My body felt chilled, put on ice, never to be thawed out ... would it ever warm enough to be touched again?

ॐ

EVEN FEELING THAT WEIGHT, I WAS CRAVING SOME SORT OF HUMAN connection. I just wasn't sure what that should look like. I wasn't one to sit around and mourn, or just sit around at all, really, so I needed to figure out a way to get out and interact with people without being in any kind of singles situation I wasn't ready for or interested in facing. I stepped back into my default behavior where it had always been easier for me to *do*, to take outward action, than to *be*, to sit at home and take in what was clearly missing – some much-needed introspection. Clearly, that type of 'doing' behavior was what had gotten me to this point to begin with, but it's hard to break those old habits and beliefs. When you've been labeled an achiever, how do you learn to *be* rather than *do*?

Intuitively, I figured the best thing would be to get out and spend time with people who would be supportive and love me unconditionally while keeping my mind occupied. I just needed to figure out how to go about doing that and who would be the people I could spend time with to help me heal, without me needing to actually ask for that help and support. Vulnerability was not yet a word that had entered my vocabulary. I didn't know how to broach the subject with friends or where to turn for the support I needed. Throwing myself into my work only took me so far; I needed to find other releases.

Baby steps, really: babysitting

There is something about children that is so endearing, and spending time with them has always made me feel happy and loved. I wanted to get out of the house and was ready for human engagement of some sort, but I also felt far from ready or interested in facing the world and the singles scene. Even though I couldn't articulate it or admit it to myself, let alone express it to anyone else, I felt in my bones and deeper the need to do some more healing. I didn't yet have the self-awareness to acknowledge that healing probably needed to come from within rather than outwards, so I looked for external distractions I thought would help me with that healing process.

Spending time with children felt like the answer. I figured babysitting was a good, safe way for me to get out of the house and do something for myself, and at the same time do something nice for friends and their relationships. Since I didn't have a relationship to focus on, at least I would be helping my friends focus on theirs by giving them opportunities for date nights. (It's not lost on me that I still wasn't yet ready to do something just for me, I still had to be giving to others as well. It would have been tragic for me to be seen as selfish or self-indulgent!) Besides, I'd always had much better luck with the two- to four-year-old boys than the boys within the two- to four-year age range around my own.

My intuition was right; the kids loved me, and I loved spending time with them. I got to laugh, giggle, play and feel warm and at peace inside. No stress, no judgment, no anxious feelings that a ball was about to drop. Spending time with the kids felt gentle and healing and was also the fastest speed I was ready to handle in terms of interpersonal interactions. And, let's face it, they were a great distraction, so I was able to escape sitting at home on my own, where I was faced with my own thoughts on being alone in my home. I have to give a hand to all the moms and dads out there, though. Even helping others out with their kids in a very *part-time* manner put me in a place where I soon felt the need for adult interaction of some kind.

One more step: Gay Boyfriends

I have always cherished my Gay Boyfriends and thoroughly enjoyed their friendship and company, but their importance in my life took on a new meaning when I became single again. They warmly welcomed me into their lives in a whole new way and always made me feel special and like I belonged. They provided exactly the right level of adult interaction I was craving. I am so thankful for my Gay Boyfriends, who were completely accepting of who I was, flaws and all. And to add icing on the cake, they often told me how wonderful I looked (and they meant it sincerely). I felt seen and accepted. They helped me feel better about myself, and the fact that there were never awkward moments at the end of the night while saying goodbye, or a question of if they would call again, was an even better bonus. With them, I could talk about anything at all and it was with these friends I felt I could be the most relaxed and real as I started to socialize again. Outside of lack of sex, these relationships were satisfying on many levels. Well, not complete lack of sex ... I did get felt up the first time I met one of my newer Gay Boyfriends.

♌

I TOOK ONE LAST LOOK IN MY FULL-LENGTH MIRROR BEFORE HEADING out the door. I felt like I was dressed appropriately for a party with a literary crowd. It was a warm night so I put the top down on the convertible, not at all worried what that might do to my hair or my appearance; I wanted to fit in, but I wasn't necessarily looking to impress anyone. I walked up to the building that housed one of my Gay Boyfriend's authors' co-op and saw people on the stairway. The get-together was already in full swing. It looked to be a mixed crowd – straight, gay and questionable.

I gave myself a pep talk. *It's okay to be here; you aren't looking to meet a guy, you are just here to support your friend at his event, so just relax. Contrary to how it feels, there is no neon light flashing on your forehead saying: 'Step away, divorcée coming through.'*

I found the host and said hello and he introduced me to a few people. It was actually enjoyable to meet new people and the conversations were lively and interesting until one of the guys I'd just met joked, "I would marry Julie just for her healthcare."

And without thinking, and before I could stop myself, what spewed out of my mouth was, "Not without a serious prenup in place!"

Looking at the shocked faces, I quickly took in just how very sarcastic, maybe even caustic, my rebuttal was. I was being bathed in that awkward, nervous type of laughter that felt forced and empty and I wondered how I could just slink away or somehow dissolve into the linoleum floor below my feet without leaving any trace of the past five minutes of conversation. Not possible. Awkward. Was everyone else feeling this so strongly, or was I just imagining it?

They say there is a bit of truth in every joke, but mine seemed to have a whole lot of *bitter* wrapped up in what may have been truth. Before I could figure out how to recover or remove myself gracefully, the recipient of my vitriol backed away slowly and ceased any and all conversation with me for the rest of the night. I couldn't blame him; I didn't like me very much at that moment either. I consciously knew I wasn't ready to date, but it appeared my subconscious wanted to make sure everyone else knew it too.

The wine continued to flow, and with a full glass in hand I struck up a conversation with another friend of the host. Looking at him, I wasn't 100 percent sure at first if he was gay (he actually gets that a lot. Months later he said to me, "The funny thing about you and I is that we are like two straight guys hanging out") so I eased into the conversation, a little more careful to watch what I was saying and not offend any more straight men. It became clear he was gay. Relief! I could stop sweating and relax into enjoyable, no-pressure conversation. Apparently, while I was scaring away the straight men I was at least entertaining enough to snag a new Gay Boyfriend. As we laughed, he raised his hands and started making a gesture like you would to turn a doorknob, then said, "You have a really nice rack; can I touch?"

Spending so much time on my own meant no one had touched any part of me in many months and I thought to myself (see, I'm already learning to keep my thoughts in my head rather than on my tongue) that it could possibly be a long time before anyone else asked to touch any part of me in any type of situation. So, why not? "Sure," I replied, and he reached out and copped a feel. He started holding my breasts like globes and jiggling them up and down. Clearly gay – a straight man would know better than to jiggle (or at least one who I would want to continue touching). His hands on my boobs, both of us laughing hysterically, I noticed the freaked-out expression on another one of my Gay Boyfriends. What on earth was causing his apparent distress? Was it just too much PDA for him or did he think I was being inappropriate or sleazy, or … ?

When the boob handling ended, I stepped aside and asked him why he seemed bothered. Always looking out for my best interests, it seemed he had been worried that the new Gay Boyfriend might have been taking advantage of my tipsiness or I might have felt objectified or pressured into something I didn't want to do. I have to say I loved him dearly for his concern and found it highly amusing at the same time. I in no way felt objectified or pressured. But rest assured, if a straight man had done the same thing, he likely would have gotten himself slapped. And if I didn't slap him but rather allowed him to cop a feel, he would likely have expected I would sleep with him, and then after I 'put out', he would likely sneak out and I would never hear from him again. *But* with a Gay Boyfriend I knew he was actually just appreciating me and there was nothing sexual about it. I was certain he would not only call me the next day, but he would be my friend forevermore. Which, as it turned out, was the case. By the end of the night, my new Gay Boyfriend and I exchanged phone numbers and kissed goodbye on the cheek to seal our new friendship.

Finding a new Gay Boyfriend proved very rewarding and came without the headaches of straight dating. The new Gay Boyfriend copped a feel and it started a relationship rather than an expectation to sleep together. And yes, he did call, and yes, it was the beginning of a beautiful, long-lasting and satisfying (on most levels) friendship.

CHAPTER THREE

A boy friend before a boyfriend

LIFE WAS FEELING GOOD — MORE NORMAL THAN IT HAD IN A LONG time. I was feeling less jumpy, I was having fun and enjoying the people in my life. But there was only so much time a single girl could spend babysitting, hanging with the Gay Boyfriends and with married friends and flakey single girlfriends that cancel. For about the third time in a row, I was canceled on for a hike, so I went on my own. Don't get me wrong, I really enjoy hiking on my own. Sometimes I prefer it. It's one of my favorite ways to clear my mind and process and figure things out. It can be an amazing form of meditation for me. Unfortunately, on that particular day I was really looking forward to some company, so I was feeling a bit sorry for myself and put out by the cancelation.

Perhaps it was time to find some new straight, single friends. Maybe they wouldn't be as flakey? But how did one go about that?

In college and my early twenties, it felt so easy as there seemed to be places where similar people congregated, but as I got older it felt harder to make new single friends, especially as fast as I had been hoping to make it happen. So what should I do? I decided the right answer was to look at online listings, of course! You could find anything on those, right? The trick would be to find someone who was in the same space I was. I wasn't quite ready to date but was ready to start dipping my toe into single life and get out a bit more. I was in that limbo land where I wanted to have more interaction with people, but I didn't want to date or be in a position where someone would consider thinking about me as anything other than a friend. I'd always enjoyed meeting new people and having new experiences and it felt like it was getting to be time to incorporate a bit more of that into my life.

Project 'Find Friends'

After my solo hike, I sat down at my laptop and set to work. I easily discovered a platonic section in online listings and checked out the 'women looking for women' as well as the 'men looking for women' sections. I didn't have a whole lot of luck in the W/W section. There was one ad that looked promising, so I replied to that, but her responses came across as a bit 'off' and perhaps not quite all there in the smarts department. I decided to take a pass.

Two M/W ads intrigued me. The first one seemed close to perfect. He said he worked in public relations and was too busy to find a girlfriend or have time to date, but often needed someone to accompany him on business outings. He wanted someone who could dress up for fancy events and be comfortable at the ballpark too. Presentable, not overly made up, able to converse with the clients, open to holding hands and a peck on the cheek here and there. He seemed to be describing me! I'd get to go out and socialize and schmooze with someone else's clients without having to actually date. That sounded like a lot of fun – and how perfect was that scenario, because I wouldn't even have to stress about the clients since they weren't my clients to worry about? What a find! It sounded like all the fun I wanted without the pressure of the events or clients impacting my own life and livelihood. And I knew I could easily help him out by impressing his clients with engaging conversation. It sounded like a win/win to me.

You may be thinking, *Wake up, Julie, that sounds too good to be true … I hear the warning bells ringing.* If that's what you were thinking, you'd be right.

I replied to the ad and explained my situation: well-educated, articulate, newly single and wanting to get out, but not wanting to date yet. I suggested meeting for coffee as I expected he would want to interview 'candidates' to make sure they really were presentable to clients. I knew I would want to do that. I felt little butterflies of excitement because I thought this could be just the type of fun I needed.

My heart may have skipped a beat when I noticed the reply had come in: "I have good news and bad. The bad news is that my company had layoffs, but the good news is my old company hired me back, so I have a job. I no longer need someone for client appearances, but if you are still interested, your picture gets mine."

The nerve – jeez. On the one hand, I had to give him credit for the clever (albeit deceitful) way of getting dates, but you would think if he could figure out that scheme, he would be smart enough not to reply to someone who specified they were not interested in dating. Or maybe he was really a predator and figured those might be the best girls to try to date as they might be vulnerable? No matter what he was thinking, I was thinking: *no longer interested.* So what did I do?

I sent my picture and said, "Sure, big boy, let's give it a go!"

Not!

I probably should have just let it go at that, but I wrote back, "As per my previous email, I am not actually interested in dating, so I won't be sending you a picture as I am no longer interested." Not so surprisingly, I didn't hear back from him again. At least he was smart enough for that. I wonder how many responses he got and if he ever met anyone this way? Maybe he's living happily ever after with some stupid girl he snagged with the fake ad!

The straight Boy Friend

And what about the second ad? That guy was a year or so younger than me, recently divorced and looking for an 'activity partner'. Not as exciting as the first ad, but with visions of flakey friends in my head I tried again. He replied quickly and said to pick an activity I liked, so I suggested a hike and we picked a date and time to go. Project 'Boy Friend' had launched!

He (*potential* Boy Friend at this point) offered to come and get me, which was thoughtful, but I suggested I should drive so he wouldn't have to backtrack to pick me up. Really, I just wanted to drive myself rather than getting in a car with a stranger, and I didn't really want said stranger to know where I lived … just in case. Always a good idea to be a bit careful.

Heading over to his place, I saw my mom's face come up on my mobile and took the call. She innocently asked what I was doing for the day. I told her I was on my way to go hiking with this guy I met online. "What is wrong with you?" she screamed. "You're supposed to be my smart daughter! (Special note to my sister if you read this: that was a joke, Mom wasn't serious!) Haven't you heard of the online killer and all those girls who got killed??? He could take you out hiking somewhere and push you off a cliff." There was a higher likelihood the ex would have thought about that than some random guy who was looking online for an activity partner – after all, it's not like he'd lived with my habit of buying more shoes than one should own in a lifetime for seven straight years.

Besides, I could have picked golfing, tennis or the movies and there wouldn't have been cliffs involved. I filled my mother in on this and gently reminded her that not only was I not a prostitute who'd placed an ad for 'massage', but *he* was the one who'd posted the ad and if he decided to push me off a cliff, someone could trace him back to the ad through the email exchange on my computer.

I pulled up at his place without giving a second thought to my mom's concerns. He was outside waiting for me; no flakiness here.

We exchanged hellos, he got in the car and asked if I could drive across the way so he could hop out at the grocery store and pick up an energy bar for the hike. Sure, no problem at all. A friendly gesture might have been to ask if I wanted one too or just bought an extra in case … but he didn't ask and returned to the car with only one bar for himself. Seemingly not a very thoughtful *potential* Boy Friend. I started wondering how promising this endeavor would be, but I was trying to keep an open mind and not judge too quickly.

Boy Friend directed me to a hiking spot I'd never been to before. I love discovering new hiking spots (I'm sure Mom would have thought a spot I didn't know = added push-off-the-cliff potential) so at least the day started looking a little more promising. We fell into an easy conversation for the whole hike and he was actually rather nice company. He was entertaining and shared openly that he was selfish – he wanted what he wanted and wasn't willing to compromise for someone romantic in his life. Fortunately, we were on the same page about just wanting to be friends. While he seemed a bit selfish, at least with his honesty about his disposition I was hoping there wouldn't be any false advertising like the last ad I'd replied to.

All in all, we had a really nice hike and morning and as we reached my car post-hike, Boy Friend said, "Mmm … I know what I'm having for lunch!" to which I replied, "Well then, you must know where we are going?!" He didn't even ask if I was okay with the spot! Rude, selfish, self-centered? He had pretty much told me he was all these things, but I found it interesting he felt so comfortable proving it over and over. On the plus side, I was able to get out of the house, he was there and ready on time and he introduced me to a new hiking spot with entertaining conversation along the way, so I guess I was okay with letting him choose a lunch spot.

The next few hikes were the same. He decided where we would

hike (introducing me to more new spots I continued to enjoy) and where we were going for lunch. He never once asked my input. Was this how he treated his male friends too? Truth be told, I didn't worry about that too much. It was actually a relief to have someone do the planning for a change (after spending my married years doing *all* the planning). Since I was always fine with his choices, I didn't feel the need to speak up. For that time, that worked for me. I realized at some point that might change and I might have the need to find my voice and make sure I was being properly considered.

After a few months, Boy Friend and I branched out into activities outside of hiking – movies, dinner, drinks. The rudeness and selfishness subsided as we got better acquainted, proving him to be a quality friend. Boy Friend was with me when the email came in from my lawyer that my divorce was final, and he took me for a celebratory glass of champagne. He'd even evolved to thoughtful!

Funnily enough, Boy Friend was one of the reasons I didn't start dating sooner. He fulfilled my need for socializing and activities. Even though, like with the Gay Boyfriends, there was no sex, other needs were fulfilled by this new relationship.

Then, without realizing the effect it would have on me, he did something that pushed away my desire to date even more. As we sat at a dimly lit bar on rickety bar stools, not yet having imbibed enough alcohol to easily erase the scene from my mind later on, he whipped out his phone and showed me the girls he'd been pursuing on an online dating app. Yuck! Dumb, bimbo-looking girls with cheesy profiles. And, of course, all tall, thin and good-looking.

I certainly didn't want to be seen as cheesy or find myself competing on that playing field! Was I going to have to continue to rely on the Gay Boyfriends for any kind of physical contact? Because if this was the way to get physical with a straight guy, it just wasn't going to happen. This online dating stuff looked way too off-putting for me – there was just no way; I didn't want to do that! Any tiny bit of interest I might have been having in online dating vanished.

While it didn't look like online dating was going to cut it for me, I started wondering what a little offline looking might be like? How would that feel? We decided to head to a favored local bar known for the singles scene. We hadn't thought through the fact that while *we* knew we were there as each other's 'wingman', other singles assumed we were together. Not that bars were necessarily the best place to meet prospective quality dates anyhow, but it turned out to be fun to go out and flirt a little. While it didn't turn into any dates, playing wingman for each other ended up being good entertainment value, and it was nice to start interacting with other single men in a harmless manner.

That continued to be entertaining for a while, but the idea of eternal celibacy wasn't resonating with me. It seemed even though I was a bit reluctant to date, if I wanted to take care of that little issue, it was time to take the plunge into online dating. I didn't stop to consider what level of turmoil and angst that would cause. I had no idea what was in store for me – so many questions I wouldn't have answers to and so many emotions I wasn't prepared for. Fortunately, intuition led me to seek out and develop a solid relationship with Boy Friend before I re-entered the world of dating because he actually turned out to be a great support. As I stepped into these new experiences, I realized how thankful I was to have Boy Friend to bounce things off while navigating dating because, let's face it, the Gay Boyfriends were only able to get a girl so far in heterosexual dalliances. Having Boy Friend's perspective on things proved enormously helpful and reassuring. This new step in our relationship took our wingman responsibilities for each other to a whole other level.

Boys and girls CAN be just friends

Boy Friend was there to pull me off the ceiling after I had my first encounter without appropriate follow-up from a guy. Of course, not without teasing me relentlessly. He liked to rub in how on most nights I had bigger balls than he had (his words, not mine), but on that one occasion I turned into such a 'girl'. Ugh, as painful for him as it was to watch, it was even more painful for me to live through because I *hated* being *that* girl. But sometimes human nature (or maybe learned behavior?) took over my mind and I just couldn't stop myself from thinking and behaving that way! Yes, I know I risk losing my feminist card when I say these things, but keep in mind, this was how I had been raised to think and it took a lot of time and effort for me to reshape those old beliefs and instill new ones.

Boy Friend was also there to remind me to be patient, which was helpful because patience was just not anywhere close to one of my virtues! It didn't help that I worked in a world where immediate response was expected pretty much 24/7. It made it all the harder for me to understand that personal life didn't work that way. I wanted what I wanted, when I wanted it, and that usually involved instant gratification – it didn't necessarily work that way in the dating world. (Those were the internal workings of my mind in a pre-Tinder world where we hadn't yet had apps training us to expect instant gratification.) It took me many years of unwinding habits and beliefs to realize neither business nor personal life should work that way and I could be much happier and less stressed out when it didn't.

Boy Friend never pushed me over a cliff. He helped soften the blow of getting back into the dating world and became one of my best friends. I had now, in my quest for getting back out there, disproved the myth that straight men and women can in no way, shape or form be 'just friends'. It can happen, even if it is a rare occurrence.

And here is where you might be thinking I am going to tell you one thing led to another and … ??? Yes, it did eventually lead to something more indeed. A decade later, Boy Friend asked me to be the best man in his wedding and I gladly accepted. I even threw him a bachelor party – it was my first, and all who participated would agree it was excellent!

While I simply went into this looking to make new friends and hadn't been searching for a Boy Friend in particular, I feel very fortunate to have developed this friendship over the years. Boy Friend has said the same. Our lives feel richer and more balanced somehow for having this relationship. I have to wonder, why don't we see more strong platonic male/female friendships in the world? Is this something we should more consciously be seeking out in our lives?

CHAPTER FOUR

Dipping my toe in

I HAD A COLLECTION OF GAY BOYFRIENDS AND A BOY FRIEND WHO I could hit the town with, but no one to date and no sex. My body was starting to wake up and was feeling ready. I don't think my mind had fully caught up with that idea, but the body was seeming to win in that tug of war. It appeared from my experiences out on the town with Boy Friend that men were somehow starting to notice me too. Or maybe I was just starting to notice them noticing me? Was I actually ready to hit the full-blown online dating scene to satisfy my body's desires, though, or was there another way? The idea of getting out there and negotiating the world of dating took my newfound breath away. Everything had changed since I was last single. I'd watched with mild amusement over the years as my single friends tried things like speed dating and spent time figuring out when was the appropriate time to return a text message and what to say. I didn't think texting for me would ever amount to more than, "Can you pick up something for dinner tonight?" I was soon to prove that wrong.

Looking backwards

The brain likes what is familiar. I learned this on the first day of my hypnotherapy training. That is why it is so hard for us to break habits and negative thought patterns, and also why, without yet having learned this information, it felt so natural and automatic to look back and revisit a past relationship when I started to think about dating. It's about choosing comfort in the known, even if it wasn't perfect, rather than fear and discomfort of the unknown in the form of online dating and meeting new men. It often gives us warm fuzzies to pull up favorite old memories of past dalliances and relationships and romanticize them, which makes it feel logical to take these experiences from the past and wonder if they could be our future.

⚄

MY TIME WITH DOUCHE BAG STARTED YEARS BEFORE I HAD EVEN met my ex-husband. I was young and single without an interesting prospect in my purview and wanted to go to a big charity party, but all my friends were going with dates. One such friend, who was newly in love, told me about a 'great guy' who was in the same boat as me. I told her (half-jokingly) to let him know it was his lucky day because if he was cute and fun, I was up for *anything* and there were no strings attached.

I got myself all gussied up in my little black dress and headed to the pre-party where my blind date awaited. As soon as I walked in, I saw a tall, somewhat dark and definitely handsome tuxedo-clad man smile and walk my way. The butterflies abounded as he stood by my side and introduced himself. It took a while for the conversation to warm up – perhaps I was taken aback by his good looks and melodic voice – but it wasn't long before there was good banter and it felt like we were both feeling the chemistry. I could hear my heart beating and was hoping it wasn't loud enough for him to hear too. He took hold of my hand as we climbed the steps to head into the party and then stopped, placed his hand on my back and kissed me gently. Pleasant shivers ran through my body and I felt like Cinderella entering the ball, but the charming prince was already at my side. Mmm … this blind date was the most pleasant surprise.

My carriage had turned back into a pumpkin long before we left the ball and then the afterparty, returning to my place around 4 am. He stayed the night, we kissed and snuggled and then went to sleep. Nothing more … no, really, he was a gentleman. At that point in my life, I was still wound tightly in morals and concerns about going too far too fast, so when I had a hot guy in my bed the first night I met him, I slept. It was years later he earned the name Douche Bag. (The name was actually spontaneously picked by a few different guys – straight and gay. I'd tell them the story and each one would reply, "What a douche bag!" I'm not kidding, each one said those same exact words.)

I woke up first and discovered it was no longer morning but midday, and I jumped when I saw how late it was. I quickly, quietly and as inconspicuously as I could scurried out of bed, picked my dress up off the floor and put it back on. His eyes cracked open. I told him to stay as long as he liked, gave him a quick peck goodbye and headed off to a wedding I was about to be late for. *Oh, to be in your twenties ... wish I could still pull that type of maneuver off!* I was half hoping he'd still be there when I got back, but I knew that wasn't likely.

℘

FAST FORWARD CLOSE TO TWO DECADES ... I'D BEEN MARRIED AND divorced, and Facebook had been invented. Prince Charming (aka Douche Bag) and I were Facebook friends but hadn't had any direct contact in years. I was talking with a group of friends about blind dates and mentioned the one with Douche Bag and how much fun we'd had. And then the lightbulb went off inside my head. We'd had so much chemistry when we'd dated, even without actually having had sex; perhaps this was just what I needed, or who I needed, to end my celibacy? Without giving myself time to reconsider, I opened up Facebook and sent him a message. A reply came in immediately and I started to daydream about what could possibly come of this.

We messaged back and forth, filling each other in on the gaps since we last saw each other, and I became one of those people who smiled giddily at my computer when reading messages from a guy. I worked up the courage to strategically mention I had been living in my place for about a year after splitting with my ex, secretly wondering what direction that piece of information might take the conversation in. Douche Bag suggested a hike. Perhaps this fairytale could pick up where it had left off and I could bypass online dating altogether? What a perfect situation that would be. The perfect romance novel.

Boy and girl have dreamy blind date but the timing's not right. Years later, after her divorce, they get back in touch and live happily ever after. The end. Ahhh.

$$\mathscr{D}$$

THE MORNING OF THE HIKE ARRIVED AND I WAS BOUNCING OFF THE walls. Was I excited, was I nervous? I was certainly fidgety in the half hour leading up to his phone call saying he was out front. I tried to appear calm and at ease as I walked out to meet him and – yikes! It suddenly struck me; this was all a bit strange and awkward! I hadn't actually thought this through to the part where we saw each other live and in person. I had no choice but to move forward; the fairytale would get even more awkward and certainly wouldn't end well if I turned and ran.

He looked good. Not as good as all that time ago, a bit older (I imagine I did too), but good. The hug he gave me was a bit more awkward and a lot less romantic than the smile from across the room when we first met. Settled into the car, our conversation was punctuated with intermittent silences. He seemed comfortable with that, but I nervously tried to fill the dead air. It had been almost a decade since I had been on a date and, in my mind, it was obvious my skills were, at best, a little rusty. If Douche Bag noticed, he didn't say anything.

After an hour or so, we arrived at the trail. As we got out of the car, I mentioned how the look of this place reminded me of a nature preserve I drove through on a business trip some months back.

Douche Bag's reply landed like a bag of concrete: "I'll be going there for New Years. My girlfriend is going on business, so I'll go along and we'll do some kayaking."

WTF???

Time stopped for a second … did I really just hear what I thought I did? Fortunately, I was standing on the opposite side of the car so he couldn't see the stunned look on my face. All I could think, besides *asshole*, was that there had been all this build-up over time and in my mind for my first date post-divorce, and it turned out it wasn't even a date?! Laugh as I might now, it wasn't funny at the time. Was this a bad omen for my future dating? And, again, WTF?!

I was trying to do the math in my head to figure out how he could have written to me all this stuff about his life, where he was living, the house he had bought, how he had fixed it up … and neglected to mention the girlfriend living in it with him. I didn't call him out on it because I was too taken aback and way too proud to let him know I'd thought this was a date. Still, I couldn't even begin to figure out what he thought it was or how his math added up. I tried to shake it off and a bit later got up the nerve to ask, "So, Douche Bag, how long have you been dating your girlfriend?"

He replied, "Five years." I commented almost under my breath that that's a long time, but he must have heard me because he followed that with, "I know, that's what everyone kept saying so I asked her to marry me last week."

WTF?! WTF?! No seriously, really seriously, WTF?! My jaw was lying on the ground.

At least we were on a single-track trail so I was behind him and once again he couldn't see my facial expression. Two thoughts were running wild through my mind.

1) How did you neglect to mention anything to me in all our many messages that you have been living with your girlfriend of five years and while we were corresponding you got engaged? And, always one for a good silver lining ...

2) I am *sooo* thankful to be the girl on the hike and not the fiancée sitting at home with a brand spanking new rock on my finger while my future husband is off hiking with some woman he went out with a long, long time ago, but doesn't really know anymore.

Jeez. Who was this Douche Bag and what was he thinking? And how in the world did I end up on this hike? Better question: What the hell was *he* doing on this hike? And which fairytale was this? It was starting to feel much more like a nightmare.

I did my best to keep my lack of composure to myself on the inside. On the outside, I graciously congratulated him and asked how they met. Online dating, of course – and the first girl he met, too. And he's now taken away *my* possibility for a perfect first date story ... unless this 'date' no longer counts?

I was a bit shocked to hear that's how they met because, from what I thought I knew about Douche Bag, I figured online dating would be way too cheesy for him. I asked about that and he told me there were basically three types of profiles: desperate, cheesy and sleazy. But in between all of those you might be able to stumble onto a profile that was more normal. Outside of the fact this guy was clearly a Douche

Bag, that gave me a little bit of hope about online dating. Not much, just a smidgen.

Even though this now wasn't a date (at least in my book), after the hike he took me to lunch at a very cute, cozy little place that was perfect for the dreary day (not referring to just the content of the date; the weather was quite dreary too). At the end of lunch, during which my mind kept puzzling over the situation more than focusing on the conversation, he slid the check over closer to him, a gentlemanly signal he would pick up the tab. I figured given the situation I'd let him do that and didn't even offer to help. Outside of the not-so-minor point about Douche Bag's fiancée, this would have appeared from the outside to be a very successful date and continuation of the fairytale. There was definitely no chance now of divesting myself of the self-imposed chastity I was feeling so ready to shed. <sigh>

Always one to question myself rather than the other person involved, I started thinking, *Am I over-reacting? Is it okay that we went hiking like this given he neglected to mention the recent engagement over the weeks we've been communicating?* Why wasn't I able to trust myself and my view on the situation? While I grappled with those questions, when hearing about it, my male friends were all quite clear: "What a total Douche Bag!" *So why wasn't it clear as day to me? Why did I still question myself and worry that somehow I got it wrong?*

Those were important questions I seriously needed to resolve but wasn't equipped at the time to process. What I didn't know then but can see clearly now is that I held limiting beliefs around what I deserved and what was available to me in terms of a relationship.

I wasn't going to be able to enter into a healthy relationship until I was able to clear those beliefs. And although it sounds romantic to create or continue a fairytale, in real life it is rare that digging into your past romances will bring into your life a strong, healthy, lasting relationship.

ℒ

FAST FORWARD AGAIN TWO MONTHS AND I WAS TELLING THE TALE OF Douche Bag to two friends. One of them said, "I know who you are talking about: _____!" How could she possibly know this just from the very few possibly identifying details I'd included in the story? Well, a friend of hers had been dating him, moved in, and when she discovered he was such a Douche Bag, my friend helped this woman move out in the middle of the night while he was away on business because she was scared of what would happen if she did it any other way. The one good thing about this story is at least this Douche Bag is off the market ... for the time being. Beware, though; I wouldn't be surprised if he strays.

Moving forward

After that lovely miss, I had to have a stern talk with myself about how looking back and romanticizing the past wasn't a path I should continue to follow. I came to the hard and somewhat frightening realization that if I wanted to explore anything – from sex to casual dating to a relationship – it was time to get back out there for real. It was time to leave the past behind (it's the past for a reason) and live in the present with an eye towards the future.

Even though the thought of entering the world of online dating was leaving a sinking feeling down to the very bottom of my stomach, it seemed to be officially time to get back on the horse. Not because I was sure I was ready to – I was definitely sure I didn't want to jump into anything serious in search for the love of my life – but really because, from my past experience, dating led to sex and it had been a *really long time* since I'd had any of that.

While the *idea* of sex was appealing, I was still absolutely terrified by the prospect of having someone new see my body naked after only one person had for nearly a decade. In my mind, it was much easier to be naked in front of someone new when you were in your thirties than in your forties. Things had started to shift and while I wasn't necessarily in love with my body in my thirties, in my mind, it looked much better back then. But I had no choice but for someone to see my naked forty-something body – if I recalled correctly, that was how one had sex and I was missing that physical connection.

I found a great Boy Friend with online ads, so as a stepping stone to full-blown online dating where I would need to set up a profile with pictures, I thought I could start looking at online ads first and see what appeared. This seemed like a more palpable next step for me. Searching for the type of date I was looking for, it turned out, could be problematic if you weren't extra careful about which section you are looking at. I did say earlier you can find anything in online ads … I learned the hard way that wasn't an exaggeration. I read and saw things that I definitely would have preferred not to see and which would be hard to erase from my memory bank.

After recovering from my horror, I found my way to the right section and quickly ended up with my first actual date.

⚲

NO BAGGAGE WAS WEARING A SHORT-SLEEVE WORK SHIRT WITH A pocket. On a date. At a wine bar. And he was clearly older than he'd led me to believe. Needless to say, first impressions were not doing it for me. Although he didn't have a pocket protector with pens in it, I was willing to bet he did before he arrived. I was really trying to be open to new experiences, but I just couldn't see things moving forward with this one. Still, I willed myself to be generous and give him the benefit of the doubt – at least for one glass of wine. After all, I did pick the place – nice and local – so I could walk over, allowing me to adjust the length of the date to the level of interest. At least it'd be a quick and easy walk home without too much time wasted. (Or, since I was giving him the benefit of the doubt, there were some nice restaurants nearby in case I magically started to find him attractive and wanted to continue on.)

I'd initially found his ad appealing because I appreciated that he called out that while we all have some baggage at this point in life, his wasn't overflowing. This seemed reasonable and self-aware. But as I sipped on my obligatory cabernet, he started telling me he was not, in fact, divorced yet. Sorry, what? He seemed incredibly bitter that his estranged wife (not ex-wife) spent – and apparently continued to spend – so much of his money. I was new at this dating thing, but I was pretty sure it was bad form to start off the conversation maligning the ex. Surely the conversation could only get better.

Nope, I was wrong. It got worse. He started telling me things that made it clear he found it an obligation and not a privilege to attend back-to-school nights and other sorts of involvement with his kids. I was confused – did this really count as having minimal baggage? I was definitely not interested in or attracted to him. There was no way this meet and greet was going to get me any closer to my new goal of finding someone to have sex with.

My thoughts started to drift away – how long did I have to stay in this situation before I could leave? Why wasn't I smart enough to have devised a plan to have someone help me out of a situation like this? I figured I'd have to rely on myself to get out of this misery. That seemed like the adult thing to do.

I had a few more sips of wine (why let that go to waste?) and decided that the close to half hour I'd been there was probably an appropriate amount of time (in my estimation, maybe not in his) to spend. I stood up and said, "It was very nice meeting you, but I can see already that we are at very different stages in our life and I think it is probably best we just part ways here. I wish you the best."

He looked a bit dumbfounded, but there wasn't much he could do. I felt a bit cruel, but I'd already endured more than I wanted to. I kept to myself the thought that he should update his ad to show how much baggage he really was carrying around with him.

Walking home, I felt a sense of empowerment wash over me. In the past, I'd never been able to just come right out and tell a guy I wasn't interested. Instead, I would continue to make excuses when they called and say I was just really busy with work. It felt good to be direct and let someone down without wasting the rest of my evening or his time.

I called Boy Friend to update him on my first date and share with him that No Baggage had misrepresented himself – he really had more baggage than most. Being the good friend he'd become, Boy Friend started to devise a plan to help get me out of future situations, but I told him not to worry because as of that evening, I'd learned how to take care of that myself.

As much as that date felt like a waste of time, I had learned a new skill that would come in handy going forward. And I felt a bit proud of myself for taking action on my own behalf and doing what I wanted rather than what was expected. On top of learning to walk away when something isn't right, I also learned that you can't know if there is chemistry unless you meet, so it makes more sense to spend less time chatting up front and meet in person to assess if there is chemistry. There definitely wasn't any physical or mental chemistry with No Baggage. I had to wonder – if he was more intellectually stimulating and our values were more aligned, would that have helped matters at all?

CHAPTER FIVE

Venturing online

I HAD A FEW MORE INTERACTIONS WITH ONLINE ADS THAT WEREN'T any more promising than the first and realized I probably needed to sign up for an actual dating site. The time had come for me to enter the realm of the cheesy and the sleazy and try to come across as and attract something that was neither.

Okay, here we go. I was actually putting myself out there, on display if you will, for the whole world to see – at least, the whole dating world. That seemed like a lot. Did I really want to do that? I felt like I had no other choice; this seemed to be how it was done these days.

Setting up my profile

It may sound easy to set up a profile, but taking on that task for the first time felt daunting. I had so many questions to ask and nowhere to turn for answers. How was I supposed to figure out what pictures to use and what to say that would get the type of guy I would be interested in to pick me instead one of the cheesy or sleazy profiles?

And if that wasn't confronting enough, it seemed I was also required to set some parameters on the type of man I was interested in being matched with. What age range did I want to set? While that seemed simple enough, I didn't actually know the right answer to that question. I figured I should be open to older and younger, and I wanted to be careful not to rule out anyone who could even potentially be a good match, so I decided to go with a decade on either side of my age. The real-life parameters I had used up to my divorce to find the right match hadn't seemed to work so well, so maybe it would help to be more open to possibilities. If I thought about it, did the parameters really matter very much if I was thinking about Mr Right-for-Right-Now not Mr Forever? In the back of my mind, I wasn't sure I'd be able to separate the two … if someone was really amazing, wouldn't I secretly hope they would turn into something more permanent?

Next up: income. I was supposed to give the income bracket I was in and the one I wanted my date to be in. I know I just said I wasn't necessarily looking for Mr Forever, but it still felt like in this area I wanted someone who was my equal. But how did I actually convey that by picking an acceptable income range for them? There wasn't a check box that said: "You must have a high income but don't worry, it's not because I'm a gold digger, it's because I want someone with a similar income range to mine." And if I disclosed my income, wouldn't that have opened me up to guys who were going to try to scam me or think that they could have a sugar momma? So how *did* I handle this? I decided to leave it blank and hope for the best.

Next up was height, weight and ethnicity … were those really the factors that were going to determine if someone was a good match? They were called 'deal-breakers'. Were they really? Or, better question, should they be? I've heard people talk about them as such, but I've also seen really happy couples that wouldn't be together if they'd adhered to what they thought their list of deal-breakers was. I really didn't want to rule anyone out based on any of those traits, so I left those blank too. These things weren't going to determine if there would be chemistry anyhow. Are there any factors outside of just meeting and seeing that can predict that?

Then it was all about me. Ugh, what was I to put in my profile and say about me? I have no idea if I spent way too much time or way too little time crafting my profile. From others I later saw, probably not enough time. The 'selfie' hadn't yet come to be and I certainly didn't have any professional pictures of myself, so I cobbled together a few I had. I wrote a fairly short and sweet introduction I hoped gave just enough insight into who I was without giving away too much or alienating anyone before I met them. It said something to the effect of: "This is my first foray into online dating, so I am not so sure how this works ... please be gentle with me. I'm looking to meet new people and see where things go, blah, blah, blah." I wanted to avoid anything that would in any way sound cheesy or desperate because I truly wasn't either of those things, and after having just gotten out of a marriage, I was definitely not yet in the right headspace to find my soulmate.

Once my profile was approved (yes, at that time that was how it worked), I almost immediately heard from about a dozen guys. This included some from quite far away, even a few different states. I'm not sure why someone from so far away would contact me? What could have come of that? While I was trying to avoid having any deal-breakers in mind, geographic desirability seemed to be one just out of necessity. Was someone really going to be willing to get on a plane to meet me, *a total stranger*, for a coffee?

More and more messages started coming in. One was from a guy who was 30 – a bit too young, but mildly flattering. And a whole lot were from outside of the top of my age range, which was less flattering and a bit frustrating. Was this what I had to look forward to? Dating men closer to my dad's age than to mine? What *hadn't* occurred to me was that by casting the net so wide I would have so many men contact me. I'd opened the floodgates. I was getting quantity, but the quality was less than desirable. I was trying to keep an open mind about all of this, but now I had to take the time to reply to all these men and it felt like a waste of my time. I wanted to be kind and reply to everyone who contacted me even though it would have been quite easy not to reply. I didn't want to be rude. And, well, what do you say to someone you can tell you aren't interested in? What was the online equivalent to meeting someone in person who you aren't interested in and politely stepping away from the conversation? I opted for thanking them for the message and leaving it at that.

In addition to finding a lot of the men unsuitable for me for myriad reasons, I quickly found out a lot of this correspondence went nowhere. Some seemed to want to just chitchat and the conversation died out before it went anywhere. Others seemed to want to just compliment me on my appearance and then it ended there. Were they just good Samaritans wanting to make someone's day a little brighter? While it was certainly nice to receive lovely messages, I wasn't a page in a catalog that required commenting on just because they looked at it. I couldn't imagine a situation where I would have wanted to say, "Hi, you are really handsome, just wanted to let you know. Have a nice life."

And then there were situations like the guy who seemed great and we planned to go on a hike, but before that happened he wrote to say his ex-girlfriend, who he hadn't been in contact with for months, just messaged him, so he wanted to cancel. Could she smell that I might have an opportunity for a date with her ex and wanted to stop that from happening? Was there going to be any chance for sex anywhere in my near future?

While I wasn't yet having any interactions I would deem successful, I was learning a lot of things I hadn't even thought to consider.

Early dating philosophies

I'll spare you the details of the first few dates that were fairly ho-hum. Suffice it to say those early experiences, along with the communications, helped me formulate a few guidelines, boundaries and philosophies. I'm sharing them here in the hopes they are helpful, but I also realize everyone needs to form their own version of these. Personally, I find it's easier for me to see what someone else has done before to help me ponder what I want to do, so here you go ...

Dating Philosophy 1

Don't waste time with too much back and forth online. Instead, just use it to learn a little bit about each other and move straight to meeting in person to see if there is chemistry. You really can't tell chemistry until you are face to face.

Time is important to me. I don't like to feel I'm wasting it, and I try my best not to have regrets about how I spend my time. I quickly learned that online communications and phone calls were often not a good judge of personal chemistry when two people meet. Some people are charming in email but have no charisma in person; some are good or bad on the phone. I spend so much time at work on the computer and on the phone, and to me the whole purpose of dating was to get out there in real life and meet new people – so why not cut to the chase and do just that?

I also learned the hard way that while this philosophy can save time, it also ups the chance of spending time with someone you pretty quickly realize you don't want to spend a whole afternoon or evening with, which leads to ...

Dating Philosophy 2

The first in-person interaction should be short, perhaps even time-boxed, like a coffee or a drink – I've coined this interaction the 'meet and greet'. (If I thought someone seemed promising, I left time afterwards so we could continue on and turn the meet and greet into more of a date if we both felt the chemistry and wanted to continue.)

To me, the big difference between a meet and greet and a date was that prior to the meet and greet you hadn't yet actually met and decided in person if you wanted to spend time with them. It moved onto a date at the next meeting or if at some point there was some sort of acknowledgement on both sides that you liked each other. More than just, "I'd like to see you again," which could be hollow words, not actual truth.

Dating Philosophy 3

Have a few conversations going simultaneously, but not so many that you can't keep track. I'd recommend putting this practice to bed when you meet someone you like and start seeing them more seriously.

I quickly learned my tendency was to get anxious about whether someone was getting back to me or not. I was able to quell that when I had a few conversations going at once so I wasn't overly focused or invested in one 'relationship' that might not ever come to be. I said earlier that there seemed to be more quantity than quality, and while that can be tiresome, the positive side of that was I could always be easily distracted by one guy if another one wasn't getting back to me. That was the attitude I needed in order to keep myself trying to meet new people, and to keep it kind of light at the beginning when I did meet someone I felt I clicked with and started to let my mind wander to what could come of it.

Dating Philosophy 4

Remember your self-worth. You deserve to be treated well. Don't let anyone treat you badly and don't take on someone else's bad behavior towards you as meaning you are any less than or not deserving. If they don't treat you well, walk away. It is their loss.

I fully admit I sometimes slipped and let it get to me; I've had to really practice and be mindful to adhere to this philosophy, but I am human, so every now and again it still stung. It's not so different than when you interview for a job you really want and you don't get it.

When I think about online ads – and I'm talking about buying and selling things, not dating – how many times do people write or call and say they want to buy something, only to never be heard from again? There are a whole host of reasons that could happen, and we never know why. Do you take that personally? No, you might be miffed, but you don't take it personally. I figured if I applied all these same behaviors to the online dating world, that would make it much easier not to take any of it too personally. The internet makes everything appear much less personal in a way, so I was quickly learning it was fairly easy for bad actors to ignore or disrespect someone they hadn't met yet, forgetting or not caring that they were real people who get hurt.

Dating Philosophy 5

Be safe. Unfortunately, in the world we live in, this seems more important for women than men, but it's important for all people. Don't give out your last name or any personal details to someone

you haven't met or are meeting for the first time. And meet for the first time in a public spot.

This is another important thing that crosses over between online ads and dating. I was always careful to make sure to keep my full identity (last name) private until I got to know someone well enough that I felt comfortable. And I would meet them in a public place and not let them know exactly where I lived. I might not have worried like my mom did that Boy Friend would throw me off a cliff, but I did take my safety and wellbeing seriously. And I always made sure we exchanged phone numbers in advance of meeting so that if it ever came to that, there was a record of their number in my phone records and they couldn't just disappear.

Dating Philosophy 6

Do your best to keep an open mind, enjoy the process and use it to learn more about yourself and what you want. Part of that is getting really clear on what you are looking for and communicating that to yourself and others. Is it a fling, a partner, or somewhere in between? And realize this might change over time and be okay with that, so long as you are clear.

The point of all of this was to have fun, wasn't it? I tried as much as I could to keep a positive outlook about it all and enjoy myself. Unfortunately, it was so much easier to say I wanted to get out of my head and have fun with it than it was to put that into practice.

Dating Philosophy 7

Look at this as an opportunity to meet new people who may or may not bring something into your life. Always try to be kind and find something positive about the other person.

Even a bad meet and greet had the opportunity to become a story to entertain my friends with ... right? Or to become a friend, teach me something new, or somehow bring something into my life, and I theirs, that made us better for having met. Keeping it positive like that helps us draw to us more positivity and more potential to find a good match.

⍥

I LEARNED SO MANY INTERESTING THINGS DURING THIS JOURNEY which helped me form these philosophies to get started. Some philosophies changed along the way as I learned more, but it was good to have these guidelines for myself. I had lots of new experiences – some good, some bad, some odd, some that helped me better understand myself, and others that helped me better understand others. Some that were hilarious, others that were mind-boggling or hurtful, and some that took a while to process and figure out what the lesson was. I am happy to have had all these experiences and opportunities for growth and learning.

I had to put myself out there and be an active participant to make those happen; it wouldn't have happened if I'd just sat on the sidelines.

The stats

What it boiled down to the first six months was online communication with about 40 new guys per month. Yes, that is a lot of communication. I was experimenting, so it was okay, but that was way too much to really engage deeply and it definitely wasn't a sustainable way to live my life. Out of all the communications, I ended up meeting about three or four men per week, ranging from 29 to 76 years old, and then ending up with a boyfriend without even realizing that was where I was headed. It was a lot. It felt exciting at first because it was new, but it wasn't something I would necessarily recommend. Hopefully you will find a much better way for yourself.

Let the online dating begin!

CHAPTER SIX

Re-loſing my virginity

NOW BACK TO OUR REGULARLY SCHEDULED PROGRAM. SEX.

My body was re-awakening and feeling ready. My mind was still trying to catch up with the idea that in order to have sex with another person, they would be seeing me naked. And touching me in places no one other than my ex had touched me in nearly a decade. Was I really ready for this? Physically and emotionally? I wasn't sure I could even picture any of this in my mind, but at the same time it was feeling very necessary. *Deep breaths, Julie, deep breaths. You can do this, it's going to be okay; with any luck it will be much more than okay.*

This time I'll remember my first fondly

Kentucky contacted me and said he was coming to the area to visit his family. I wasn't quite sure what to make of someone who was looking to set up a date before they were even in town. Was he real? Was he a scam? Was he really coming to town? Was he in a relationship back home?

I liked what he had to say in his profile, so I set my concerns aside and decided to go with it. I wasn't sure how attractive I found him, but Kentucky seemed witty and interesting and he said he was intrigued by my profile, so why not? We exchanged mobile numbers (I saw mobile phone numbers as safe since they weren't tied to your name or where you lived) and continued to text now and again until he came to town.

As soon as his plane landed, Kentucky messaged me to let me know he was in town. Up until this point his messages had been fairly PG, but now they became a bit risqué. Was this standard procedure when a person arrived in town and was setting up a meet and greet? I didn't know. I hadn't experienced this with anyone in the past, since the last time I was single texting didn't exist yet. Or maybe I should say sexting, as this was kind of in that realm. He would write something suggestive and I would nervously try to maneuver back to PG by answering with something evasive and non-descript. I didn't know this guy and had no idea how or where messages I sent him could resurface. There'd been plenty of instances in the news about that kind of thing, and while I wasn't a celebrity or a politician, I did take my business reputation seriously, so I was careful … and a bit shy and naïve about this type of messaging, too. I wasn't very sure of myself or if this was all okay. Then Kentucky sent a message that felt a little *too* over the top. As I sat there staring at my phone trying to figure out what to do, I got another message to the effect of, "Sorry about that, that came out creepy."

Could he feel my uneasiness coming through or was it my lack of a quick reply that tipped him off? Whatever it was, I reasoned that since he'd figured out the creepiness factor on his own without me pointing it out, he might be okay. Besides, in general, he was also funny and witty and I have a sweet spot for that. I wasn't yet fully acquainted with how all of this worked ... was I being too conservative or was he going too far? I guess we'd soon find out.

_ℒ_

I WAS ALREADY SEATED AT A HIGH-TOP TABLE WHEN KENTUCKY walked in. We had arranged for a post-dinner drink at a bar close to my place. Right from the get-go there was chemistry, and I could tell by the way he was leaning in that he felt it too. Yes, finally! I still wasn't sure if I found him handsome, but his personality was great – less in that "oh he is such a nice guy" way, and more in the "hmmm, this could be interesting" kind of way. This was so totally different than the previous meet and greets I'd had. Easy banter, enjoyable conversation; I was finally having fun and focusing on the conversation rather than calculating how much longer I needed to stay so I wouldn't be rude.

We were much more interested in each other than the drinks and we each nursed a single drink for the few hours we were there. I hated for it to end. I finally had to pull myself out of it and suggest we call it an evening as while Kentucky was on vacation, the following day was a workday for me.

Kentucky asked if he could at least walk me home, explaining he wanted to be a gentleman and make sure I got home okay.

Against my better judgment, I let him.

Maybe I should have been a little more careful about letting a stranger – one from out of town, no less – see where I lived, but I trusted my intuition and sensed it would be okay. The bigger issue was once we got to my door because, to the best of my recollection, there were not many gentlemen who *only* wanted to see a girl get home safely. If I remembered correctly, seeing a girl home was more about a kiss and an invitation up to her place.

Cockblocked by my brain

At this point in life, I no longer had my virtue to protect (although in my mind I'm not wholly sure I'd let that one go), nor a roommate or parents waiting up for me. Could I find any plausible reason or excuse for this situation to end at the door? Did I want it to? That sex and connection I'd started to crave sounded great in my imagination, but now that the reality of it was standing on my doorstep, I wasn't entirely sure my head had caught up to my body's desires and I wasn't sure how to progress it along.

I have absolutely no clue what we talked about the whole way home. He could have easily been speaking gibberish or a foreign language as far as I was concerned because I was so up in my head, thinking, *Okay, now what? How do I handle this? What do I do? This is what I have been thinking I want, but this is really a strange feeling! What am I going to do? What should I do? What shouldn't I do? What does he expect? Does that matter? What do I want to do?*

The thoughts were still swirling in my head as we got to my door. *Maybe I should have picked a place that was further away to give myself more time to think. I don't want him to see my panic; that would be embarrassing.* I finally managed to pull a few thoughts and words together and got them to come out of my mouth. "I am guessing you want to come up right now, but this is all new to me and to be honest, I am really not sure what I should do here."

Oh, the charmer that Kentucky is, damn him, he had the perfect response: "Let me just step back here for a minute, then, and give you some space to have a discussion with yourself. When you figure it out you can let me know." Ah, wit and charm always get the better of me. Did he know that? Did he know he needed to coax my mind into catching up with my body's desire?

It worked. That did a good enough job breaking the ice and relaxing me a bit so I, still with a bit of trepidation, told him he could come up but just for a few minutes. (If you are thinking, *Yeah right, just a few minutes, uh-huh,* I was kind of thinking the same.) Sitting on my new sofa, in my new-ish home, was the first potential suitor I'd had and it was a man I'd only just met. It was so many firsts for me. Even though we were just sitting there talking, it felt extremely awkward and I was feeling quite shy, which wasn't my usual way of being. *Could he sense that? Did he feel that? Is that why he decided to start giving me a back massage? To ease my tension?*

I was pretty certain that wasn't why. And knowing that, I involuntarily reacted by cringing or at least tightening up at the feel of his hands kneading my shoulders. It wasn't that I didn't want them there – it was because this experience was so foreign to me. But, of course, he didn't know that. It didn't deter him, and we managed to move from back massage to kissing to full-blown make-out session. Even though I began to relax and enjoy myself, I stopped there and kicked him out so I could get some sleep before heading off to work a few hours later.

Now don't get me wrong, it wasn't that I didn't like him, or that it didn't feel good, or that I was frigid in any way; it had just been so long since someone other than my ex (or Gay Boyfriend, who doesn't really count in this matter) had their hands on me that it felt really strange. At that moment, strange = uncomfortable! It was clear where he wanted to go with it, and maybe if I hadn't been so self-conscious about someone new seeing me naked and preoccupied with how strange it felt, I could have let my mind go and enjoyed it, and we could have ended up with him in my bed. But once again, although my body was ready, my mind had been programmed differently for so many years – it needed more time to catch up.

Even with all the uneasiness, I felt more alive and enjoyed the chemistry and connection. It felt really good to wake that up and know it was possible to feel those things again. That was definitely the most successful meet and greet for me at that point in time. I think in Kentucky's mind it may only have been a partial success … although points to him for not pushing the matter.

The next day, the flirting and light sexting continued. I sat myself down for a little woman-to-woman talk with myself and realized Kentucky was the perfect answer to completing my mission to have sex without getting attached or jumping into a relationship. *Think about it, Julie; you have real chemistry with this guy, you enjoy spending time*

with him, he's a good kisser and gives a nice massage, he is right in front of
you and available and you don't have to worry about getting emotionally
attached or wanting more because that isn't possible – he doesn't live here.
So why don't you just relax and have a little fun?

From celibate to casual

Apparently, my pep talk worked. I found myself making plans for
him to come over for an afternoon. There was a lot of tension building
up in the following few days with all the texting and planning for
his visit, so by the time he arrived at my house, all the agonizing over
someone seeing me naked again seemed to be long forgotten. And
yes, it would appear that having sex is like riding a bike: it all comes
back naturally when it's time to go for a ride. I have to give it to
Kentucky – losing my 'post-divorce virginity' was a whole lot more
fun and satisfying than losing my virginity the first time around. But
much like the meet and greet, this date came to an end before I would
have liked and still left us each arriving late to our late afternoon
commitments. Objective of having sex again: check! With a smile on
my face and a glow in my cheeks to match. Yes, the Gay Boyfriends all
commented that something was different and that I looked fabulous
when I finally arrived to see them.

✄

HERE'S THE BIG QUESTION AND THE ONE THAT WEIGHED HEAVILY ON
me and left me feeling a bit anxious after the afterglow wore off the
following day: just what is the appropriate follow-up after casual sex?

This was new to me. I hadn't been in this situation before. Sex was always something that was part of a relationship or on the way to a relationship, not something entered into so soon or so casually. When Kentucky left the previous afternoon, we'd said we'd get together again, and I was looking forward to that. But I wasn't getting the level of follow-up I was expecting, and I started to go back to my old mindset and habits. I felt anxious about what it all meant and what would happen.

All those fears from my teenage years – the thoughts of having sex and never hearing from a guy again – resurfaced. Plus, I'd enjoyed it and wanted to do it again … and had limited availability while Kentucky was still in town.

Boy Friend to the rescue! I called him up and told him I needed a distraction, so we went out on the town for the evening. I was clearly anxious, though, and he was truly amazed to see me "acting like an anxious girl" for the first time since we had met. Ugh, it felt as terrible as I'm sure it looked. What was it about me that I wasn't better at taking these things in stride and letting them roll right off me?

My rational mind told me to do that and knew it was the best thing to do, but hormones or chromosomes or something took over and possessed me and I no longer had control of my own mind or emotions. I hated that feeling so much! I've talked to girl friends who have experienced the same thing and felt the same way. (While this may not sound like the best description for gender equality, it is just how I felt, and I haven't spoken to men who've experienced the same – although I am sure there are some who have.) I guess it was helpful to recognize that these weren't rational feelings or behaviors, but acknowledging that didn't make them go away. All I could think was, *Please, someone put me out of my misery and make this horrible feeling I can't control go away!*

$\mathscr{D}$

KENTUCKY EVENTUALLY CAME THROUGH AND WE MADE PLANS TO get together again. Once again, we didn't go out, we just stayed in. I was perfectly happy with that. We had no time pressures that time, so he even stayed the night. I enjoyed spending that time with him: good conversation, good chemistry, good sex, good everything ... but no chance of anything more than a fling since he lived in another state. Was that part of what made it so good? I'm not sure. Even if we lived closer, from his point of view I don't think anything more would have been put on the table. I got that, and at least on the surface was good with that, but it kind of felt like a shame that we wouldn't be able to get together more often.

While I accomplished my goal of re-losing my virginity, I was disappointed Kentucky's time out here would come to an end without me getting to see him again. We did text a little bit over that week, but that was it. I had been hoping I would hear from him again after he left and maybe see him on another visit, but he didn't offer any of that up. I wasn't so sure how good I was going to be at casual flings. <sigh>

I will always fondly remember Kentucky as my first ... my post-marriage first. And I will be forever grateful he came into my life the way he did, at the time he did, and for how he guided me back into so much I had shut off for so long. He was witty, charming, fun and totally unavailable … which was probably a good thing, or else I might have started wanting more. Like it or not, that's how my mind worked.

Quite frankly, as much as I really liked Kentucky, I suspect he would have been a terrible long-term relationship guy, at least for me. I would have liked to have a bit more fun with him, though, and would have been open to meeting him somewhere for a long weekend rendezvous every once in a while, but he didn't seem open to that. Perhaps he suspected I wouldn't have been able to remain *detached*, or maybe he was actually *attached*.

For all I know, Kentucky was actually in a relationship and just sneaking around with me even though he claimed to be single. Silly to go down that path of unknowns; best to take it all at face value and be thankful he got me over the "I can't be seen naked" hump (yeah … that pun wasn't intended, but there it is anyway) and opened me up (that pun wasn't intended either) to being excited about a guy and realizing I can go out there and have fun. He helped prepare me for the anxiety of not hearing from someone when I hoped to, and helped me learn that that's part of dating – even though it certainly isn't the fun part. And even saying that, if I'm completely honest, there is a part of me that wanted him to want more and held out a glimmer of hope he would. Why was that? Habit of thinking that way and wanting to be wanted? Underlying old belief that if there was sex there needed to be more? I'm not 100 percent sure.

Good ol' Kentucky, I wonder where he is now …

CHAPTER SEVEN

A string of entertainment

I TOOK A LOOK AT MY PROFILE AND DECIDED IT NEEDED TO BE rewritten. "I'm new to this, be gentle with me" wasn't how I wanted to come across any longer. I wrote myself a somewhat more provocative headline: "I've been told I have nice ..." And once someone opened the profile it continued: "I'll let you decide what that is when you meet me." It seemed to work like a charm as it gave guys an easy opening line (some were much better than others). And that gave me a chance to evaluate how witty and smart they might be. I updated my photos, too, so I'm not sure if that helped more than the words or vice versa. To be clear, the photos I added weren't provocative, just the words were more playful. I didn't want to show sexy photos with too much skin – I know others did, but I didn't want to compete with those or be evaluated or compared based on those types of photos either.

Why the update in profile? I valued and enjoyed the wit coming from potential suitors, so what would it say about me if I didn't offer up the same and have an entertaining and intriguing profile? It seemed to get the guys' attention. A few were also humored by the short messages I wrote. I guess many of the other women wanted more talk, but for me the messages served one purpose: making a plan for a meet and greet. I didn't want or need for a guy to 'get me' via email or vice versa. I wanted to figure all of that out live. Long, drawn-out online communication was boring to me. I didn't want to spend more time at my computer reading their entire life story. I just needed enough insight to entice me to meet them and feel fairly confident the odds were in our favor we'd have a nice meet and greet.

Unfortunately, even with all the attention I was getting with my new profile, none of it felt nearly as interesting or exciting as Kentucky. I definitely had the post-fling blues and found myself daydreaming about getting together with him again. No, I wasn't stupid enough to be dreaming of a relationship with him, I just continued to think about and romanticize meeting up for a continuation of the fling.

New guys and messages continued coming in almost daily. If I'm honest, just seeing what new guys were checking me out and communicating with me became a bit intoxicating. It was fun and exciting – often more exciting than the actual meet and greets themselves. I was still trying to stay open to meeting guys I couldn't necessarily picture myself dating. I didn't want to limit the playing field to a 'type' and rule out someone who might turn out to be interesting.

There were some messages that were just sooo bad, I couldn't even bring myself to meet them.

My parrot and I just happened across your profile and I was
inspired to say hello. I am a single male attorney ...

Seriously? This came from a man with lots of education if he was
an attorney. Could that ever have possibly gotten a positive reply?

Then there was one I am not even sure was for real, because who
in his right mind would choose the name he did unless in real life he
actually was a doctor whose parents named him Richard Shrivels? If
it's a real name – lord help that man! And his parents, too ... what
could they have been thinking? Dr Dick Shrivels?!

Now I do have to admit, on my shallow side, if either of these guys
had been drop dead gorgeous, I may have given them a chance to meet
in person just to see. But, alas, that wasn't the case for so many of the
guys who didn't present themselves up front to be nearly as interesting
or witty as Kentucky had. He'd raised the bar and I wasn't ready or
willing to lower it.

On the plus side, there were some witty responses that intrigued
me. After a message or two back and forth I got:

From here we could ...
Introduce ourselves
Continue to chat here
Have a night of wild passion
Call and talk (his # inserted here)
Live happily ever after
... I'm thinking a subliminal message ... Your choice.

Now that one seemed witty and charming and reeked of possibility, yes? To redeem myself from the earlier shallow comment, I should point out here that this guy was a bit older than I would normally be interested in and didn't even have a photo posted. So, wit and charm could be as appealing, if not more appealing, than a hot bod and seriously good looks. Really – I mean that! Unfortunately, I never got to find out what was behind the wit as he just dropped off and I never heard from him again.

That seemed to happen a lot. While it was disappointing, I *tried* to never take it personally. I was mostly successful with that but not always. I've spoken to women who continually allowed it to cut them deep, and felt bad for them. But if I was being smart about it, why would anyone allow that? And this goes for both women and men who are being treated poorly. With online dating, you don't even know the person yet and they don't know you, so it makes no sense to take it as a personal rejection. Yet somehow it seems hard for us as humans with feelings not to.

For all I knew, some of the guys behaving this way were married and just getting off on flirting anonymously online, or they were writing the same thing to multiple women and got another response before mine and were focusing their attention on that, or they got called out of town for a long business trip, or, or, or … The list goes on. As much as I desired closure, it was impossible to know what happened, so I endeavored to do my best not to worry about it. I just moved on to the next one and chalked it up as not meant to be. Maybe the universe was looking out for me and helping me dodge a bullet from an unsuitable guy who would have had no positive impact on my life.

It is only fair to mention that on my end sometimes I started to communicate and just never got back to the guys too. It happened in both directions – not just the men doing it. My reasons varied from a busy week at work, too high a volume of communications to deal with them all, loss of interest in the communication, or deciding the guy didn't seem interesting or appropriate in any way. Take your pick; it could have been any of those reasons. I'm not proud that I didn't always close out communications in a respectful manner. If I got to the point where I met a guy in person, though, I would always let them know I wasn't interested in seeing them again if they tried to communicate with me after a meet and greet. I did my best to always be nice and respectful; I never wanted to intentionally hurt anyone's feelings. Unfortunately, there are a lot of people who don't seem to have the same values or take others' feelings into consideration.

The quantity of messages I was receiving was flattering, but the quality was overall a bit lacking. <sigh> You've heard the saying "The odds are good but the goods are odd"? Welcome to my online dating life.

Even still, before I knew it, I had meet and greets lined up one right after the next. It kept me busy and entertained, and truth be told, it kept my friends even more entertained as I amused them with the tales of my online dating correspondence and meet and greets that led, mostly, absolutely nowhere. In online dating, it seemed you had to kiss a lot of frogs …

Gay Straight Guy

His message read, "Let's get together to talk about our dating experiences and *EPL*." My first thought was, *What is this guy talking about?* But then I saw it was in his favorite book list. *EPL* stands for *Eat, Pray, Love* – a classic chick-lit book. Was this guy even straight? Maybe he was listing it as a ploy to try to sound sensitive. I couldn't help but feel that meeting to talk about dating experiences and *EPL* sounded more like a girls' night than a recipe for a successful meet and greet. I mean, I know I was trying to stay open to dating different types of men, but …

I forced myself to stop judging him and give him a try. Maybe he was nice and just what I needed.

He skipped hello and started our meet and greet by remarking, "Your pictures don't do you justice!" I know this is meant to be flattering, but I'm pretty sure this is just a line. I'm harder on myself than anyone I know, and the pictures I'd finally selected for my profile represented me well – I didn't think I looked any different in person. Maybe it was actually code for, "Oh look, you have big boobs, I didn't see those in your pictures!"

I expected we would start by talking about *EPL*, but he went straight into dating experiences – oh joy. "The women are so flakey," he said. "I know that can happen before you meet, but my last girlfriend I met online just disappeared. She stopped taking my calls and I don't know what happened."

Hmph. I'd known this guy just a few minutes and I was pretty sure I knew what had happened. He went out with this girl a couple of times and thought she was his girlfriend – but she thought she was just getting to know him, decided she didn't like him and didn't see any point in continuing. I opted to politely keep this thought to myself, which gave him all the room he needed to continue.

"What bothers me more is when women use the excuse that they met someone else and wanted to see where that would go when I know they really just don't want to see me again. If that's the case I shouldn't still see them online. Right?" Sounded reasonable enough to me – I couldn't argue against that at all. At the same time, I could understand how that could happen. Gay Straight Guy seemed so earnest I didn't want to hurt his feelings either. I mean, I already knew I wasn't interested but I felt bad ending this already. I didn't think he could tell how I felt – I bet he couldn't tell with those other women either and continued to pursue them. Poor guy just wasn't good at reading the room.

I had a feeling this would go on forever unless I ended it, so I decided it was time to practice my new skill. "Thanks so much for the coffee, I'm sorry we didn't get to talk about *EPL*, maybe next time?" *Shit! Did I just say that? I don't want a next time, how did I just do that? Ugh ... I can't really take that back, can I?*

"I'm so glad you said that," he said. "I've enjoyed meeting you so much."

Before I could think of a way to remedy the situation I'd inadvertently created, Gay Straight Guy enveloped me in a big hug and smacked an enormous messy smooch on my lips. Yuck. I felt like a toddler whose crazy relative wants to smother them with affection but they just want to be left alone. Couldn't he feel my body stiffening up or see the shocked look on my face?

"How about brunch on Sunday?" he asked.

Nope, he certainly didn't notice and still couldn't read the room. I did NOT enjoy being hugged or kissed by that man. Maybe I could ease him into transitioning from potential love interest to friend when we met for brunch?

I didn't think Gay Straight Guy could shock me more than he did with that hug and kiss, but he did. The day of our intended brunch 'date' he contacted me to let me know he needed to cancel because he had met someone else and "wanted to see where that would go". Wasn't Gay Straight Guy the guy who, just a couple of days before, had told me he *hated* it when women did this to him? But it was okay for him to do it to me? Not that I had actually wanted to date him, but still, did he even realize his own double standard? He still had his profile up and I could see he was checking it daily. Seriously?

I was more amused than hurt because I wasn't interested. Gay Straight Guy's double standard was odd and off-putting, but not nearly as odd as him contacting me a few weeks later to see if I might still be interested. Really??? No response warranted and none sent. I made a mistake I paid for with that one. I needed to be clearer and more up-front about my lack of interest on the spot. Lesson learned the hard way. Was there another lesson I missed here, though? Should I have called him out on his double standard or was that unnecessary and the kinder thing was just to let it go?

The Interviewer

I liked The Interviewer's profile when I came across it, but from what I'd experienced so far it seemed the guys liked to reach out first, so I decided to park it and see if he contacted me.

It worked!

"I can see from your pictures and profile you have a nice ... a lot of things ... Check out my profile again. If you are interested and would like to meet, let's get together. Face to face is always a lot better than trying to learn via email."

After Gay Straight Guy and a few other dead-end meet and greets, this felt pretty normal, honest and interesting – and he was cute, too. On the downside, he didn't seem very worldly and exciting, but maybe a little more honesty and less excitement was what I needed. Maybe a good guy would be good for me?

The night of the meet and greet, I was tired – it had been a long day at work – but I had a good feeling about him. I finished applying my lip gloss and got out of the car. I could see him standing in line. He was still cute in person; that was good. But ugh ... we were standing in line to order our food? This was barely a step up from a fast-food place. Definitely not a place I would have selected.

Okay, Julie, relax, take a breath, be nice, I told myself. *You don't really have a choice in the matter so make the best of it.* I ordered a burger and fries and even after I offered to chip in, The Interviewer insisted on paying. I was inwardly pleased he was a gentleman. Brownie points. Yes, I know its old-fashioned, but I still think it's good form on a first date for the guy to pay ... I do always offer, though.

I had plenty of time to munch on my fries while The Interviewer gave me an overview of the position he had available. I hadn't realized I'd be interviewing for the role of 'wife' five minutes after meeting – that wasn't discussed in the arrangement for the meet and greet. Did I miss a memo? I got it; a relationship ending in divorce wasn't what he'd signed up for and he didn't want to be alone. It sounded nice that he just wanted someone to love and adore, but did I really want to know that before I even got to take a bite of my burger?

I wasn't sure this was a position I wanted to apply for. The problem was, I was already there and my default mode is to interview to get the job – I have a pretty good success rate. He was cute and seemed like a genuinely good guy. I really wanted to be attracted to the good guys. I'd had more than enough of the crazy or unsuitable types … maybe I should just go for it?

The questions kept coming: "What does an ideal weekend look like to you? How close are you to your family? Do you have a big group of friends?" I felt like I was giving all the right answers and I was nailing this interview. But I'd been interviewing candidates at work all day and this felt more tiring than engaging. I was not finding this fun or relaxing – I felt like I was still at the office, not at a meet and greet.

For what felt like the millionth time, The Interviewer responded to one of my answers with, "Wow, you are really impressive, and I find you very attractive too." Was that nice or odd?

I couldn't keep my inside voice inside my head any longer and I finally blurted out, "You know, this kind of feels like an interview. I've been doing those all day, but they only last for an hour."

I held back a chuckle and hid my look of dismay as he said, "Oh, that's okay, you don't have to worry, I don't have to stop at an hour." Points deducted for lack of sense of humor and self-awareness. <sigh>

He told me one more time how impressive I was, this time adding that he'd definitely like to see me again, and I realized the interview had finally come to a conclusion. Nailed it! But had he?

I was really wanting to give the good guys a chance, but should I have to work so hard to convince myself to want to see them again? The Interviewer quickly followed up the meet and greet with a message saying, "Thanks for the great get-to-know-you date last night. I was impressed by you and your experiences in life, not to mention your exceptional good looks." Wanting to convince myself I should go for the good guy, I replied and agreed to see him again. But that was it. When I checked there were no further messages. The Interviewer went from fawning over me to going so far as blocking my profile overnight! I certainly hadn't seen that one coming. Was "you are so impressive" code for something else I wasn't aware of?

It seemed even the seemingly good guys exhibited some pretty bad behavior. Why was that? What lesson was I meant to take away from this experience? "Beware of the seemingly good guys because they might not actually be good after all"? Or maybe it was "if a guy doesn't seem like a fit, don't go on a meet and greet with him because that's not a good use of your time".

Hair Vest

Hair Vest's English was so broken I struggled to understand how he was a writer by profession. I understood English was his second language, but really ... he must have worked with a really good editor. He pushed hard to meet me "as soon as possible" but that just was not going to happen; my dance card was pretty full for the next week. Still, it was somewhat endearing that he kept texting me good morning and intermittently throughout the day saying he was thinking of me. The longer messages required a bit of decoding due to the broken English, though. And I wasn't as sure as he was that the fact I was at yoga while he was at the gym and we both had sushi the same day were signs this was a match made in Heaven. I guess we'd find out.

If the weather was any indication of how the meet and greet would go, I was in for a good time. It was a beautiful morning and, score, there was one last outdoor table at my favorite coffee shop. It was a good morning. Or maybe not ...

I saw a man approaching me who looked similar to Hair Vest's pictures in his profile, but this guy was definitely at least four inches shorter and not nearly as attractive. Did he post pictures of his better-looking, taller brother? Or maybe it wasn't him? He smiled and waved. I looked around ... yep, that was definitely aimed at me. <sigh>

If only that was the extent of the problem at hand, this meet and greet might have been salvageable. But no, on this beautiful day, Hair Vest was wearing a zip-up sweater that apparently got stuck below his chest. There was no T-shirt under said sweater, only his extremely hairy chest on full display for all of us in the vicinity to experience. His decision on where to stop zipping made this sweater lower cut than anything I ever dared to wear. I resisted the urge to shade my eyes from looking at him straight on. It was sooo distracting. I wasn't sure I could have a serious conversation with Hair Vest. It was taking all my willpower not to reach over and pull the zipper up to a respectable, non-laughable position. Ugh.

The universe can be kind and it can be cruel. I was starting to curse my luck at getting an outdoor table as I felt the eyes of all the passersby on the sidewalk lingering on Hair Vest. I knew I had no one to blame but myself for this one; I'd got myself into this situation. And it appeared I would not get out unscathed, because along came my nice, sweet neighbor waving at me. Fortunately, she said hello and just kept walking. Phew. But still, what did she think of me sitting there with this man?

Just when I thought I'd dodged the proverbial bullet with a full-blown conversation, I saw out of the corner of my eye an old friend I hadn't seen for years. Normally I'd love to say hello but at that moment I was trying to make myself small and invisible so she couldn't see me. She still saw me and came walking towards me. *Shit!* I might not be the vainest person about my own looks but the idea of anyone thinking Hair Vest was my date or, even worse, my boyfriend was turning my cheeks red. Maybe I'm a terrible person but, what can I say, the visual of that hairy chest on display was not pleasing – it was embarrassing.

I don't think there is a nice way to say, "While I am really happy to see you, please don't think any less of me for this; I had no idea a man would show up for a meet and greet with his hairy chest inappropriately displayed. Oh, and this is only a meet and greet, don't worry – it won't lead to a date." If I could have slithered under the table and disappeared, I would have. But my friend stopped to talk and introduced me to her friend. I was dying a little bit inside because I knew the polite thing was to introduce Hair Vest. But I really couldn't call him that, could I? And I couldn't introduce him by name either because I wasn't sure how to pronounce it. I was fairly certain the situation would get even more awkward if I asked him or pronounced it incorrectly. Ugh, once again, this was not fun.

After my friend left, I didn't think it could get any worse. But Hair Vest gave me the requisite comment about how my pictures didn't do me justice, continuing on with, "My ex-girlfriend is a Brazilian swimsuit model and I've dated many beautiful women and models in the past." And this was important for me to know at that very minute because …? Was he wanting me to know he had dated women far more beautiful and superior to me? As I was pondering this, he said to me, "I know from your messages you wake up early, but you better not wake me up that early in the morning unless it is for sex, and even for that you should let me sleep a bit later." Wow, this one had a vivid imagination.

He seemed to be immune to the unimpressed and pained contortions of my face as he continued telling me about dates we would have in the future, complete with sexual innuendos which were neither clever nor welcome. "And if you are a good girl and don't wake me up too early, I'll give you the breakfast of champions to suck on." The only thing keeping me from pulling my hair out or screaming was the disbelief that seemed to have rendered me temporarily frozen in place. I was shocked and horrified by what was coming out of his mouth.

I finally shook it off and came to my senses. I told him I needed to go. I didn't share that I didn't actually have to be anywhere else, I just felt like I needed a shower after listening to his filth.

As we parted ways, Hair Vest said, "I've shown you I'm interested, so now the ball's in your court, you contact me if you want to pursue this."

"Don't hold your breath" seemed a bit nasty, so I just smiled and thanked him for the tea. I held in the laughter until I was half a block away and he couldn't see me. OMG, the hilarity of the whole experience. I couldn't stop laughing to myself as I thought it was good he'd left the ball in my court – because it was going to stay there!

Not too surprisingly, the ball didn't get to stay in my court. Two days later, I got a text from Hair Vest saying, "You are good girl, but not one for me. Good luck." Clearly, he didn't understand the meaning of "the ball is in your court".

I was left feeling heartbroken and dejected. What have I got left to live for? ;-)

Another lesson painfully learned. Do not set up meet and greets anywhere you can possibly be seen in public with someone you might not want to be seen with, no matter how convenient the location might be for a quick and easy escape!

The Pilot

A girlfriend a few years older than me asked if all my dating was through online means or if I had done any "dating in the wild". Dating in the wild? What's that? Apparently, it's when you meet a guy offline somewhere and he asks you out on a date. According to her, that didn't happen much anymore, and I would have to agree. I was getting more attention than I could handle through the online dating channel, but dating in the wild just didn't seem to be in the cards for me. I wasn't sure why. And then, of course, because we talked about it, it happened! Well, the meeting part, not necessarily the dating part.

✆

IT WAS THURSDAY NIGHT AND I WAS HAVING DINNER WITH A girlfriend. The conversation turned to the dating slump (plenty of meet and greets, none interesting, and no sex involved) we were both experiencing and we decided it might be time to see if we could end the dry spell. We opted for a popular dance spot for a post-dinner drink. As I ordered our drinks, I noticed a guy down the bar staring at me. I smiled and looked away and when I looked back, I could see him watching me. He wasn't trying to hide it. The Pilot and his friends inched their way over and bought us another round of drinks. We talked, we laughed, we danced. It was clear The Pilot had set his sights on me and his friend was making moves on my friend. We joined them and their group of international pilots and their crew who were in town for two days. The night went on with more drinking, dancing and flirting. Before we knew it, it was last call and the bar was closing down around us.

My girlfriend turned to me and whispered, "He's invited me back to his hotel room, what should I do?" We excused ourselves to the ladies' room so I could give her a pep talk.

"Screw the moral dilemma, I thought you wanted to end your dry spell?" I'd had far more drinks than my normal, so the answer seemed obvious. She wasn't fully convinced so I reminded her she could change her mind at any time and decide to put an end to things. She didn't need to do anything she didn't want to do. Ending her dry spell was her prerogative – just remember to use protection. That seemed reasonable enough to her. Decision made; problem solved.

The Pilot and I headed out and stopped at the liquor store for a bottle of wine to take to his room and continue the fun. Why I thought this was necessary or a good decision, I'm not sure. I'm not a very good drinker and I'd already had more to drink than was likely to leave me in tip-top condition the next day. In this situation the idea seemed like the logical next step, so I went with it.

The Pilot leaned me against the wall in the elevator. We fumbled and stumbled a bit due to the drinks, but it still felt romantic to be in an elevator kissing a handsome pilot I'd just met. He stopped kissing me long enough to tell me how amazing I was and invite me to his 40th birthday party halfway around the world. And then, after another kiss, he asked me to spend the following day with him. Smooth … his method of seduction was intended to make me feel he wanted me for more than just the deeds we were about to perform.

I was adequately charmed and taken in, but for some reason also very preoccupied with wanting to see his uniform. I wanted to be sure he was a real pilot. He opened the closet and I saw it hanging there, perfectly pressed. I stumbled over and looked at the pins – turned out he was the captain. I'd found my proof, but we couldn't find a corkscrew for the wine. How to solve this dilemma? He kissed me and told me to hold tight as he went to the front desk to find one. I can only imagine what they thought, having just seen us stagger to the elevators when he returned for a corkscrew. Soon I'd have to walk back by them as I made my way home. Oh, walk of shame, how you haunt me! The only good news was I wasn't dressed like a hooker so hopefully I wouldn't get kicked out and asked to take my wares elsewhere.

The Pilot returned and opened the wine. We had one sip and he kissed me again. I was enjoying this but also giggled nervously as it sank in that I'd never really been in a hotel room before with someone who I hadn't intentionally checked in with and known for more than a few hours. Out of nowhere, I found myself compelled to ask, "So what have you got going on back at home?" Earlier he'd told me he was single, he definitely wasn't wearing a ring, and he'd just invited me to come visit him halfway around the world and go to his birthday party, yet still I pulled that question out.

"Well, I am married and have a little boy."

Stop! Say what??? Okay, nice meeting you, time to go!

I may have been testing out being easy, but I was not willing to sleep with a married man. I couldn't help myself, I had to ask: "If you have all that at home, why are you here with me?"

"I've never done this before, really, you are just so beautiful I couldn't stay away."

Awww, so sweet and romantic. NOT. Not when you are married, anyhow. Yuck. And even if I was born yesterday, I still wouldn't believe this was a one-time thing. No one is that beautiful. Well, maybe someone like Salma Hayek, but even if there is someone that beautiful, that someone is certainly not me. I gathered my things and started making my way out.

"Can we still hang out tomorrow?" he asked.

Why was he throwing that one in there? Did he think it made him sound sincere and I'd decide to stay? I may have had more than my limit of drinks, but I still had my wits about me enough to decline that offer too. I had my heels back on and my coat over my arm as I started towards the door, but his voice stopped me.

"Wait, before you go, can I just touch your breasts? They look amazing."

This wasn't a Gay Boyfriend in the making, so in my mind there was only one plausible reply to that request: "You're right, they are amazing, in fact they are absolutely spectacular." I turned and walked away down the hall without looking back.

My dry spell continued.

CHAPTER EIGHT

Still learning

DRY SPELL ASIDE, I WAS LEARNING A LOT ABOUT MYSELF — AND ABOUT others, too. I was still questioning myself more than I probably should have been. Was that part of the process of discovering who I was and wanted to be? Or was it the remnants of my past programming? Maybe it was just that it was hard not to question myself when I was getting mixed at best and deceitful at worst messages from the men I was meeting? I seemed to continue to have more questions than answers.

One thing I was finding was that when I didn't have a good connection with the men I meet-and-greeted, I tended to wonder if it was me. Why wasn't I able to connect with this seemingly nice guy who, on paper at least, seemed to be a good match? Was I just not capable of forming the sort of connection I wanted?

When I was in the moment or replaying the meet and greet, I questioned myself. Now, when I step outside of myself and think about it more rationally, I can see it makes sense. While I don't believe there is only one true match for us in our life, I also don't think there are hundreds or thousands, so it would make sense that I wouldn't and shouldn't feel that connection very often. But in the moment, in the situation, I couldn't escape the feeling that something was wrong with me for not feeling the connection.

There was still so much for me to try to figure out, like how to separate physical chemistry from genuine connection, and how young was too young when the chemistry was sizzling and, most importantly, whether I was even capable of feeling the sort of passion I was beginning to realize I was worthy of feeling.

I had to wonder, if I trusted myself to make better decisions about the men I've been involved with throughout my life, would I be able to come up with answers to all these questions? Perhaps the scars from those relationships that ended in me being hurt or deceived had formed so deeply on my psyche I was not yet able to see clearly what I needed to see to know who I was and what I wanted. With each new interaction, I was learning more and peeling back more and more layers, undoing programming and limiting beliefs that were still handicapping my love life.

Is it me?

My mother likes to tell the tale of how she just wanted to have her own baby to love and cuddle and then I came along and wanted nothing of that. There is an entry in the baby book she started working on from the moment I, her first child, was conceived:

1 ½ years old. Julie is horribly sick. For the first time she wants to be held and cuddled.

Maybe it's just me and how I'm wired, but I've never been a fan of, or completely comfortable with, outright displays of affection. So I've never in my life understood what possesses someone to want to sit next to you at a table at a café or restaurant rather than across from you where you can see each other and carry on a proper conversation. Seriously, what? I just don't get it. It even makes me a little uncomfortable when I see other people doing it. And when it's me doing it, it's definitely not by my choice and it's just plain awkward. When I see couples like that at tables, it's all just too syrupy sweet. Can they really not stand to be further away than that from each other for even the course of a drink or a meal?

I think that's why I had problems letting my guard down with Romeo Side Sitter – I was the first to arrive at our meet and greet, and when he turned up, after a kiss on the cheek and a hand up and down my back (already a bit too much touching too soon), he settled in next to me so close that our legs touched. "I can sit on the other bench if this one is more comfortable," was my nice way of saying, "Back the F up, Romeo!"

"But I like it here next to you," he said, grabbing my hand. Squirm. Already it was just too much PDA for me even if I was in a relationship – let alone in broad daylight in a coffee bar with a guy I'd met not even five minutes ago. The only reason I stayed was because it didn't feel overly sexual and imposing – more just that this overt affection seemed to be his nature.

I wonder if this particular aspect of his personality brought my own into stark relief. Is that what both attracted me to and repelled me from Romeo? There was something fun and exciting and passionate about him that captured my attention. Tolerating his overly ambitious PDA definitely pushed me outside of my comfort zone – somewhere I'd been trying to consciously take myself. It made me feel uneasy, and at times a little anxious, but I kept thinking maybe there was a lesson to be learned here.

After tolerating the meet and greet and warming up to him more over phone calls and texts, the first date itself left me feeling no more physical chemistry than I originally had. Romeo was a nice enough looking guy, definitely in good shape, well dressed and presented well (although a touch shorter than me … don't judge me, I'm already judging myself!) and capable of planning good dates at nice places, which I was finding few men were skilled at. I couldn't decipher if it was that I wasn't physically attracted to him, or if his level of touchy-feely-ness was pushing me away rather than drawing me in. The second date (dinner, coffee, dessert and sitting in his car at a lookout point where I totally missed the fact we were meant to be making out) left me feeling worn out – that's a long time feeling uncomfortable. His suggestion of salsa dancing was the final straw. Rather than visions of sexy salsa, I had visions of my bed … alone.

All the right elements were there, yet I just couldn't take one step further outside of my comfort zone. Would I have been more open and willing to push myself if he was the right guy for me? Was it a genuine lack of connection holding me back, or was I just too scared to take the leap? I wish there was some way to know. And I wish I could have just let myself go and run wild with him and enjoyed him for all he was. But something stopped me. Was it me, or him?

I sometimes wonder if things would have turned out differently if he'd had the patience to wait to see if I could develop the passion and interest in him that he was so ready to shower over me. Or even if we'd met a few months later when I might have been more open to such attention, thanks to my 31-year-old fling.

So that's what chemistry feels like

Ahhh, 31. Just when Romeo Side Sitter had me worrying if I even *had* the ability to feel such passion for anyone, this oh-so-young and so-not-my-type hipster sent me a message. *What does a 31-year-old, tattooed, hipster, smug, sarcastic guy want with a corporate gal my age?* That's the first place my mind went when I read the message from 31. But then I thought ... *Okay, he looks like he might be kinda cute and appears to be smart and witty, so I'll play along.*

It was easy from the start, with his text suggesting a happy hour drink coinciding nicely with the end of my commute home and a rare free slot in my calendar. Although I didn't know the bar he'd suggested (a mix of hip and divey, dim enough to create atmosphere and leave you not 100 percent sure of your date's attractiveness in the light of day) and the conversation started off a little forced and awkward (possibly because I was self-conscious about the age difference), after we each had a drink we relaxed into the meet and greet. So much so that we decided to continue on and we both called to cancel our back-up plans – I guess the back-up plan is something that spans all generations!

As we got up to leave, he leaned over and kissed me ... It wasn't bad, or even awkward. It didn't even feel like too much too soon, even though I'd known him at that point for under an hour. In fact, it felt quite nice.

From that first kiss onwards, in the cab, at the next bar and then the restaurant, 31 seemed to always have his hand on my leg or my back, in constant contact. But somehow it felt right, barely noticeable – quite different than with Romeo Side Sitter where it just felt uncomfortable and too much.

I guess I had my answer. It all boiled down to chemistry.

Who knows what possessed me to open a bottle of wine when we got back to my place? His age, his looks, his charm? My Mrs Robinson ways? I'd had more than enough to drink that I don't remember all the fine detail, but the clothes came off, fun was had and 31 stayed the night. The next date was planned before he left.

We hadn't yet gotten to the second date and 31 messaged me asking if he could stop by for a short 'visit'. I was again serendipitously home and free. Having someone in the area who could drop by was proving much better than the distance between me and my friend Kentucky. Definitely a fun way to spend a rainy weekend afternoon.

So began my exploration of a 'friends with benefits' relationship. He proved to be a little flakey, but outside of Kentucky I'd never really had this kind of 'relationship' before, so maybe this was just what was to be expected? I guess reliability and respectfulness aren't necessarily part of the equation, but as long as I'm a willing party that's okay, right? Or is it? No one has ever educated me on the 'rules' surrounding this sort of thing … if they even exist.

When I was in my twenties, my grandma said to me, "Honey, if you can't be good, be safe."

And I told her, "Grandma, believe me, I am good and I am safe." It was more talk than action back then, but after all these years of being the good girl, I think my time had come to drop the good and just be safe, right? (From my vantage point, the correct answer to that question is a resounding YES.)

After not hearing from 31 for a few weeks (yes, that left me feeling a little anxious and unsure even though this was something casual) he sent a text: "Still have those tan lines?"

I figured flirting was in order to fully hold his interest and replied, "Hmmm ... I'm not sure."

In my mind, the reply to that would be, "How about I come check?"

I was not at all expecting a reply of "Check and let me know." What the hell was that? Was he a little slow? No longer interested? Why was he texting me then?

I simmered down and replied, "It might be more fun if you checked. What do you think?" Phew, the flirting worked and garnered an invitation to his place, where we settled in for a glass of wine and some tan line exploration.

So where did this go from here? Obviously it couldn't go too far, right? It was fun but not earth-shattering, and while he was closer than Kentucky, he wasn't close enough, reliable enough or frequent enough to make this a nice, easy, regular occurrence. Should I even need to really give it much thought? It was what it was, right? A once-in-a-while flirtation and afternoon or evening of fun. I still wasn't sure what I was looking for at that point in time, or if these interludes even *needed* to go anywhere, for that matter, but even so, this sort of thing still left me a little uneasy.

It turned out I didn't have to give it too much thought, as a few weeks later he got a new job and moved away. Before he moved, we got together for a lunch and a dinner and did just that – shared a meal and nothing more, no tan line exploration. We were seeming to transition into a nice friendship, and we stayed in contact now and again over the years. In fact, we've moved on from monkey business to doing a bit of business together. Who says sex *always* ruins friendships?

It's not always clear-cut

It had only been a few months since I'd started my dating experiment, and I'd already progressed in leaps and bounds. I was in the process of *learning* to let go of the attachment between sex and relationship – that deep conditioning I was struggling to overcome. I say learning because it wasn't like I didn't have setbacks where I started imagining what could be or feel anxiety when I didn't hear from a guy I wanted to hear from. But while I had setbacks (that is how we grow), more significantly, I determined I was still capable of feeling passion and physical chemistry (just not with short men who sit too close) and developing the connection I had feared I wasn't capable of. It felt empowering to find that part of myself and feel a bit more *normal*.

Just when it all started to feel a bit more clear-cut – either there was physical chemistry or there wasn't – Man-Boy came along to confuse me all over again. I felt like I was in a game of ping-pong between my head and my heart ... and other parts down lower. Which part of me was the rational part and which part was making decisions?

Man-Boy didn't fully capture my attention at first. I wasn't sure I was interested in him, but he singled me out so strongly I *wanted* to like him and agreed to a meet and greet. He was the right age demo but came across a little nerdy, and the way he described his life bounced back and forth between coming across as a full-grown man and an adolescent. When I thought we were just halfway into our meet and greet, he abruptly announced he had to go back home to do some work. Was this his way of saying he wasn't interested in me? I was bothered by that idea even though I wasn't even sure if I was interested in him. Old patterns can be so hard to break.

The evening ended with a hug that might as well have come from my brother. A bit awkward, as little touching as one could have and still call it a hug ... and no chemistry. Not that I want chemistry with my brother, but on a meet and greet it would help. As we were parting ways, he said we should definitely get together again, and although I hadn't felt any chemistry, I agreed because ... maybe he did actually like me and maybe that could develop?

He planned a nice date at one of my favorite restaurants, which made me feel hopeful, and I started romanticizing what might come of this ... even though I wasn't yet certain I liked him. It would appear I didn't need a man to give me mixed messages; I could do a number on myself with them! I was putting way too much thought into this way too soon. I had often advised others to steer clear of this behavior, but I seemed hard pressed to take that advice on myself. Intellectually, I knew I needed to get out of my head and let things just unfold without attachment to outcome, so why was that so hard for me to do? Was I able to do this more with Kentucky and 31 because they weren't suitable matches or remotely available, but when someone more 'appropriate' turned up, I regressed to old thoughts and behaviors?

Before the date, I tried on outfit after outfit and I couldn't decide what to wear. Nothing in my closet seemed to be conveying the right combination of confidence, sex appeal and a casual I-haven't-overthought-this look. Man-Boy smiled when he saw me, so I took that as a sign that the final outfit was the right one. We walked into the restaurant and, just my luck, of all the restaurants in the world, we were at one with a co-worker and his wife seated at the next table, close enough to easily overhear our entire conversation. We took our time so the table next to ours turned over and we could talk more freely. Man-Boy seemed a bit taken aback by our new table companions – a very pretty transvestite with a dapper older gentleman. He kept sneaking looks her way and later asked if I noticed. I told him I hadn't because I had been paying attention to my date. Hint, hint. At least he insisted on paying for dinner even after I offered to help.

Since Man-Boy wouldn't let me pay for dinner or drinks at the wine bar, I thought it polite to invite him for one last glass of wine at my place. He looked around my place and was quick to comment on how neat and clean it was ... a few times. On top of living in a tiny studio, was his place also a messy/dirty studio? Note to self: Do not go to his place, it might make me not like him anymore (not that I was yet sure whether I liked him or just his choice in restaurants).

He continued looking around, to the point it was borderline creepy – what was he searching for? I must have looked at him funny because he told me he was just being curious. Yes, I could see that; I just found it odd. He even pulled my Netflix DVDs (remember those?) out of the sleeve to see what I had. Good thing I didn't have anything incriminating. But who does that without even asking? I wouldn't even do that at a close friend's house.

Then, all of a sudden, Man-Boy said, "Come here." I moved closer and the next thing I knew he *threw* off his glasses (a little dramatic, but okay) and kissed me. I was quite surprised by his boldness; I had pegged him as a somewhat passionless slow mover and thought I might not even get a kiss goodnight, or there wouldn't be chemistry. I definitely misread the situation. I will spare you the salacious details, but it would have been good if I had planned ahead and gotten a bikini wax – oops.

So there we were. What next? What was I feeling? Was this too much too soon? Would I not hear from him again? Did that matter? I still wasn't even sure if I liked him, but when the physical chemistry was good, it confused my logical brain. *Did* I like him? Did I like the chemistry? The biggest question in my head was still whether he liked me. Why was that question still at the forefront instead of the background? As soon as the clothes came off, I seemed to turn into a girl with crazy unnecessary thoughts! I was left wondering *Will he call?* instead of *Do I want him to call?* Was it time to have my head examined?

I went out with the Gay Boyfriends the next night and a good time was had by all. At dinner I regaled them with stories of my previous evening and Man-Boy's excellent oral skills – in fact, I was worried mine were not as strong. The Gay Boyfriends, as always, were ready to help a girl out. They gave me some pointers on how to best use your hands and mouth in coordination, shared some of their own experiences and told me about the book *Sex Tips for Straight Women from a Gay Man.* Sold! One of them loaned me their copy (not sure why they had it, outside of emergencies like this), and I read it cover to cover.

Everything I read I already knew about or was so far out there I didn't think even gay men would likely partake. (I checked this out with one of the Gay Boyfriends later and I was right.) I did pick up a few 'finesse' pointers, but in general, nothing new. Maybe porn would be a better instructional tool? Another Gay Boyfriend suggested gay porn; he said most women like that better.

And then I played the waiting game. I definitely wanted Man-Boy to call, but I wasn't sure if that was more because I didn't want him *not* to call or because I was actually interested in him. What troubled me about the idea of him not calling was this: I had him pegged as a good guy, and I wanted him to follow through and *be* a good guy so I could be sure my intuition was right and I could trust it.

Man-Boy finally called a few days later. I was relieved. He *was* a good guy, he did call. He liked me and I could relax. Except on the next date I began to realize I actually didn't like him that much. The chemistry seemed to have disappeared. Was alcohol a missing ingredient or was I finally realizing that just because someone liked me, I didn't need to like them back? Relief: my decision was made. I was clear; it didn't matter what he thought, I definitely wasn't interested in him.

But then ... he didn't call. Which should have been okay, right? Because I'd already decided I didn't like him. But instead, I started wondering why he didn't like me and felt upset that he wasn't calling! Why was I torturing myself like this? Why couldn't I just decide if I liked someone or not without any consideration for if they liked me back? Yes, I frustrated myself to no end with this type of behavior. It was hard for me to let go. I kept thinking about Man-Boy. Was that because I was getting to the point where a relationship seemed more interesting than dating around? Or was it just because I didn't want to be rejected? How was I meant to separate the two and figure that out?

CHAPTER NINE

Pay attention to the warning signs

ALL THINGS CONSIDERED, I'D HAD A GOOD RUN SO FAR WITH ONLINE dating. I'd met some good men, had some sex, had many funny experiences and kept my friends entertained with the stories. Most importantly, I was starting to learn a few things about myself. Just starting ... I knew I had a long way to go. I still needed to figure out where my boundaries were with some things, what I really wanted and, most importantly, why – when I knew logically I should be worrying about whether *I* liked *them* – I still spent more time thinking about whether *they* liked *me*.

And here's a new revelation: how quickly and easily I got addicted to attention from prospective matches and missed it when it slowed down. There was something about the possibility of something new, something to look forward to, that was enticing, and I was getting greedy. I wanted more of it; it was like a fix I needed on a regular basis. I guess it made me feel a bit like a schoolgirl ... and what's not fun about having guys to constantly flirt with? But it wasn't so good when the number of matches slowed down for a week or so and, instead of taking a break, I lowered my standards. That made no sense of all, but that's what I did. The lesson was, while it all made for good stories to keep my friends laughing, casting such a wide net so I could feel good about giving different types of guys a chance wasn't serving me well and I deserved to be dating guys that were better suited to me.

What follows are some lessons I learned (and some I hope *they* learned) on some painful dates I would have been better off skipping. Hopefully you can learn from the error of my ways and they can save you some time and energy!

Noah

This guy had "Warning: stay away" written all over him. It was a slow week dating-wise and I was curious as to why young guys kept wanting to meet me. Especially a young, single dad who lived an hour away and seemed to have his son a great deal of the time. Here are some of the warning signs I didn't heed:

- Right from the start he sent two messages at a time like he was loading pairs of animals onto Noah's Ark.

- The messages were hard to follow and the grammar and spelling were awful.

- He would rather watch *American Idol* than have a first phone call.

- He wanted to go to Chili's for dinner (yes, I am a food snob, but that is barely a step up from fast food and not even a place I would stop on a long road trip).

The list goes on from after the meet and greet – yes, I'm still shaking my head that I actually proceeded to the meet and greet. Here are the first two messages he sent me, exactly as he wrote them. In the first message, Noah is referencing what I had written in my profile, the whole message is from him:

You wrote: I've often been told I have a nice ...
Me: I have a nice ass too, cool
You wrote: I'll let you fill in the blank when we meet. If you are still reading, you are playful and have a sense of humor, that's good. Keep reading if you are looking for someone who ... Is optimistic in a very realistic manner. You can dress up or dress down. Works hard but makes time for fun.
Me: You forgot to mention that your really fine and gorgeous in your photos. I'm up for drinks too or even just going for a lunch and some tanning on a beachside bench. Anyways, tell me more please.
Thanks,
Noah

Five minutes later, without a reply from me, he sent a second message:

Nice ass
Yo,
I'm sorry, I love adlib, I'm loving the emails, please tell me more.
Your photo looks like I'm talking to you in person right now, therefore, I would like to get to know you in person over email and drinks fo sho!

Had to send a shout out, your nice!

Love,

Noah

Warning Will Robinson, warning. Yes, I should have stopped things after the first pair of messages came in, but the following week he wrote to let me know how excited he was to meet me and that his kid would have a sleepover with his grandma so we could go out. Ugh, I couldn't really back out after that, could I? <sigh>

The warning signs continued right from the minute we met:

- The minute we met was 30 minutes late because he got lost.
- Those 30 minutes standing on the street waiting were better than the first 30 minutes of the meet and greet.
- Dinner conversation was awkward, and I had as much trouble following what he said as what he wrote.
- It felt like perhaps we were from different planets and spoke different languages.

Fortunately, by the end of the meet and greet it seemed Noah wasn't any more interested in me than I was in him, so it seemed complete disaster was avoided. Phew.

But I was wrong. Two more messages came in later that night. He got my name wrong and the spelling mistakes continued.

First message:

Dear Julia I enjoyed our conversations about travel the most.
Please cut and paste the link below to see.

I have to give you a vote of confidence and tell you my reaction
to last night. First of all, when I got to the restaurant I
thought it was amazing, but destracting and it took a long
time for my eyes to adjust. When I first saw you with your tan I
thought you were an amazing woman. I didn't quite expect that
and appreciating what you have comes easy for me. Overall, the
only way to describe my impression is that you are by far the most
beautiful woman I have ever been graced to have dinner with.
The music and noisyn ess of the place made it hard to get a true
impression of your personality, but you were bubbly and laughed
alot which I liked. I hope that you may leave the door open for a
second excursion where I can get to know you more clearly and you
can get to know me more clearly in the day, and not showing up on
the fly. Perhaps a early morning cappuccino when your bored and
neading some good conversation and a walk somewhere with a vista.

Fondly always,

Noah

PS

PS,

I would love to be given the chance to woo you slowly over lunch
or coffee over the next few months, even if nothing comes of it,
it's nice to get to know someone you find attractive for various
reasons, but not all reasons, becuase there is too much I don't
know. Anyways, thanks again,

Noah

The second message came in a few hours later:

```
?!?
?!?
Didn't get a response, would love to take it slow,
fondly always,
Noah
```

Should I be flattered and/or scared? It's strange how two people could go on the same meet and greet and come away with two such polar-opposite impressions of how the evening went. I decided the best choice was to send a very firm but nice message explaining I wasn't interested and the journey ended here. I wanted to be respectful but make it clear there was nothing more going on. I didn't expect a reply, but I got one – well, technically, I got two.

First message:

```
Well, I'm dissapointed. I didn't feel like that was the right
place for me to give you my full attention and the right time
because I forgot about my appointment in the studio. I suppose
I wish you were a french woman, because then you might be a bit
more open to getting to know about the nature of all men's love
and heart and more about getting to know eachother on a creative
personal level. Anyways,
     One morning please consider, If you are ever , ever just at home,
and just up for a nice cup of coffee and a walk on the beach, please
think of me,
     fondly always,
     Noah
```

The second message came in as a PS to the first:

PS

I guess what I'm saying is that I wish you were a french woman
because then you might be open hearted and open minded into a
type of love for men you didn't previously experience.

I didn't respond, probably because I am not a French woman?! If
you understand these messages, can you please explain them to me???
But my lack of response didn't stop him from trying again a month
later, oddly, for the first time, with just one message:

Hi,

Your still the most beautiful woman I have ever had dinner
with, are you open minded and open hearted enough to do a horse
back ride with a group of five and a leader this weekend? I'm
going, would love to get to know you more,

fondly always,

Noah

If only I was smart enough to learn my lesson here and be more
selective in who I communicated with, but alas, I wasn't ...

The Loner

The Loner seemed more 'normal' and more age-appropriate than
the last encounter. But who wouldn't? His first message showed a bit
of wit, there were no spelling errors and I could understand it:

Ok, ok ... you have me interested! Well, I'll have you know I've
been told that I have a nice ***... so I guess we're even! For us to
learn about each other's secret, we'll indeed have to meet. Take a
look at my profile, such as it is, kick the tires, and let me know if
you'd care to meet up. Hope to hear from you.

This meet and greet was better than the one with Noah, but not by
much. Here are a few things I would warn a guy against if they'd like
to move on to a date:

- The first piece of information you reveal about yourself
  shouldn't be: "I don't have many friends and spend a lot of
  time alone."
- Definitely don't follow that up with: "I didn't really date in
  high school."
- And then: "I started dating in college only because some girl
  came after me."
- And the real kicker: "I was a late bloomer but I'm making
  up for it now."
- Don't pick up the check and ask for $8 for the glass of wine
  your meet-and-greet partner drank after explaining you
  have a great job and make a lot of money.

The Loner followed up the next day with a message saying he had
a nice time with me. Reading the message just made me feel tired and

worn out. Aren't communications like that supposed to at least put a smile on my face, or at best make me feel like a giddy schoolgirl? None of that was happening here. Why was it that the ones I didn't like always followed up and wanted to see me again? Was there a correlation here? Did I just not like the ones who were interested because they were interested, or was it that I just didn't have chemistry and that was okay? More for me to ponder.

Honest Abe

"Your profile intrigues me ... hmmm what could it be."

Short, sweet, pretty good start, so I replied: "The only way to find out is to meet me."

It started out well, but it went downhill from there with Honest Abe. Here are some of his faux pas:

- Asking multiple times how long I've been on the dating site – not sure why guys ask that; what does it tell them about me and aren't there better questions to ask?

- Asking if I would actually show up for the meet and greet – that sounded a bit desperate, and if I was the type who wouldn't show up, how likely was I to be honest about that?

- Telling me that he was like a Swiss train – I'm guessing he was meaning he'd be on time, but that's a Swiss watch, and I looked it up: Swiss trains are often late.

Now, one thing I liked was that Honest Abe suggested that when we meet, if either of us was "not feeling it" we should just be honest about it. I was totally up for that. I would rather have someone say "this isn't working for me" than "I'll call you" when they know they never will. And why do so many guys do that anyhow? From what I've been told, a guy doesn't want to hurt your feelings by saying they are not interested so they just say they will call. **For all the guys (and gals if you do this too) reading:** actually, that is worse, and it is cowardly; please just be direct in a respectful way. Don't get my number or say you want to see me unless you really want to and plan to follow up. Otherwise simply say "thanks, goodbye" at the end of a meet and greet. Honest Abe called this point out more than once. Was Honest Abe just really into honesty? Or was he trying to get out of this before we even went on the date? At that point I was feeling more lukewarm about this meet and greet than ever and thinking that unless Honest Abe really surprised me when we met, his honesty and keeping-it-real policy would work well for me.

The universe seemed to be conspiring to save me from this meet and greet I wasn't looking forward to. As I was driving to meet Honest Abe, I looked over to see a really cute guy in a car next to mine. He smiled at me; I smiled back. He kept smiling and looking; I smiled and laughed. This continued to go on as we made our way down the road and stopped at the stop signs. I was thinking to myself, *This guy is way cuter than the date I'm about to meet ... but what do I do about it?* And the responsible side of me said, *Doesn't matter, you have a date set up and four minutes to get there on time.* I tried to mind my own business as I was driving; he pulled up alongside me and smiled again, then got behind me and slowed down and made a left turn into a parking lot. I was kind of hoping he'd go to the same place I was or follow me. Perhaps I played it a little too coy. Could I have looked more or encouraged him a bit more?

But really, what does or should a person do in that situation? I did what was expected and arrived on time to my meet and greet. That was seemingly the wrong decision ...

Lessons that were learned on this meet and greet:

- Perhaps Honest Abe really did mean Swiss train because even though he said he was always on time, he was late.

- Providing pictures from when you are a good 40 pounds lighter makes it hard for a meet-and-greet partner to recognize you.

- Check your nose for danglers before you leave the house or at least before you get out of your car.

- It apparently is possible to talk with your mouth full, and while it's bad to see kids doing it, it's worse when it's an adult and it's the absolute worst on a meet and greet.

- When talking with said full mouth, don't ask me all the same questions that were asked and answered via text prior to the meet and greet.

- I should have made Honest Abe's question about if I would show up a self-fulfilling prophecy and gone off with the cute guy from the drive over.

> • It's hard to make conversation with someone who is likely a nice person, but who does not interest me in any way, shape or form.

As soon as I could, I stood up and said, "Well, shall we call it an afternoon?" This didn't leave much of an opening to disagree.

After giving me a hug goodbye, Honest Abe said, "We should do it again some time," and I said nothing, just smiled.

I know he said let's keep it real and say if we are not interested, but does the smile and lack of words count? It's really hard to say to someone's face, "By the way, you seem nice enough, but I'm just not feeling it and don't have any desire to see you again." It can also be presumptuous to think *they* want to see *you* again. At least I didn't make any promises I wasn't going to keep. I never heard from Honest Abe again, so he definitely *didn't* hold up his end of the "let's be honest" conversation. Although maybe that was because of my lack of a warm reception? I didn't give it another thought, but I did keep thinking, *What if, while I spent the afternoon with Mr Wrong, I let Mr Right drive away?*

Perhaps My Dear

"Good Morning Love, I see you're early bird. How are you this fantastic morning?"

His messages were peppered with calling me "love" and "dear" and every other line was "perhaps" this and "perhaps" that.

"Somehow I feel that a girl like you might be booked on weekends :) Kidding. Rain check is no problem. Perhaps if this weekend is not working for you, then we'll keep in touch. Next week I am going on vacation. Hope that no one will snatch you by the time I return. Perhaps we can catch up then."

He was a bit old-school in his way of communicating as messages continued with "of course my dear", "yes my love" … Not quite my style, especially from a stranger, but I figured perhaps we should meet. If I was smarter, I would have gone with perhaps we shouldn't. There were a lot of things not to do on the meet and greet with this one too:

- Be so timid you can't find a seat in the bar and move us over to a bar devoid of people except for a few senior citizens.

- Bathe yourself in so much cologne I swear I could taste it and was literally choking on it.

- Ask juvenile questions like "What's your favorite color?"

- When I ask what you do for work tell me "man's work" when you work in an office … does that make me a man too?

All of that happened in the first 10 minutes of meeting. I decided to pull the plug. I'm guessing that may have been one the shortest meet and greets in the history of meet and greets, but I wasn't really interested in lingering just to be nice. There didn't seem to be a point. Was that terrible of me? In my defense, I was in quite a foul mood from his sexist remarks and cloying cologne.

As we were parting ways, Perhaps My Dear asked me, "Can you at least say this was the best worst date you have been on?" How does one respond to that? I giggled (awkward laughter, not funny ha-ha laughter) and wished him well.

The next morning, I got a message from Perhaps My Dear reiterating the same thing and suggesting *perhaps* we could try again. I figured it was best perhaps to leave that one to rest and not reply; that didn't stop him from trying again a few months later.

Secret Agent Man

This one took cryptic to the next level.

"Hi Agent 5661

I read your Profile. Yes I am 'playful and have a sense of humor', although I don't know how reading your first two sentences proved it …"

He then went on to say that I mentioned one of his favorite places in his profile. Huh? Was that cryptic or a typo? I was reading this and thinking, *What??? What is this Agent 5661 crap?* Was he trying to be funny or was he insulting the profile I wrote? He didn't sign his name or ask me out, or really say much of anything. I was a bit annoyed, but I took the bait and wrote back asking if he cared to identify himself. Clearly, he didn't …

"I'm just some mysterious spy like you. I thought I would let you be the one to … 'fill in the blank'. I sensed that you were tweaking my 'playful' vibe, meaning I sensed a fun personality. But when I rubbed my eyes and reread your Profile to figure out why, I read contradictory assertions and dot-dot-dot, like a riddle inside a mystery inside an enigma. Baffled!"

Now *I* was left rubbing my eyes ... was Secret Agent Man trying to be funny, intriguing or just insulting? Still not sure.

I received a few more odd messages from Secret Agent Man, then radio silence. Okay, whatever. And then ...

"Hey Mystery Agent 385. I dropped off but now I'm back. Still top secret, as ever. Still a blank to be filled in ... Only a face to face will solve this ... maybe. Care to meet for coffee? I want to know how mysteriously sphinx-like you truly are. Mr X"

Still no actual name from Secret Agent Man. Upon our final message before meeting, he did sign it with his actual name. He was at the café when I walked up and my first thought was, *Attractive enough, especially for his age.* My second thought was, *I can't believe what a hypocrite I am – I hate when people tell me that same thing!*

Secret Agent Man was far less cryptic in person than he had been in his messages, but there were still a lot of do-nots that happened. Do not:

- Continue to interrupt and speak over me to the point where it appears you aren't listening. Not sure if this was a personality flaw or if he was just hard of hearing. Either way, he certainly wasn't picking up on my frustration with that.

- Neglect to notice my discomfort when you are gushing about how wonderful I am.

> • Talk about all the things we will do together in the future, including where we could go on vacation together, within five minutes of meeting.

Really, it seemed Secret Agent Man didn't even know I was there – he was simply planning his life with whatever warm body was sitting in front of him. This all seemed to be more about him than about me; I felt like he hadn't actually gotten to know me and would have said the same things to anyone, really.

I was still a little surprised when I didn't hear from Secret Agent Man again. Why would someone talk about all these things they wanted to do with you and then not contact you again? I actually asked him, and it turned out he thought I wasn't interested so he was taking a cue from me and didn't follow up. Hmmm … he wasn't necessarily wrong, but how much time do we spend assuming what the other person is thinking rather than just asking?

Mad Scientist

This one was persistent – so persistent he finally wore me down – and against my better judgment (why was I not learning?) I agreed to a meet and greet. Honestly, this was mostly so I could swap meet-and-greet stories with the girlfriend I was having brunch with the next day who also had a meet and greet planned … I know, I know, not very optimistic, and unfortunately, as it turned out on my end, perhaps a self-fulfilling prophecy.

The Mad Scientist suggested we meet at 9 pm. Already a bad sign to me – that's when I want to wrap up if things aren't going well, not when I want to get started. He was hidden away in a dark corner of the wine bar when I arrived ... I don't think anyone was actually meant to sit there. Odd. He didn't want to move to a nicer location even when the waitress suggested it.

And now comes another lesson on what not to say at the beginning of a meet and greet:

- "I'm from another country but I don't like the people from there, so I won't have any of them as friends here."
- "I've been searching for the perfect bar to go and drink by myself."
- When I say I don't drink much, reply with a look of sheer disappointment, "What do you mean you don't drink often?"
- "I love to drink, but I don't do drugs."
- "I only take Prozac® and Wellbutrin®."
- Go on and on about how you prefer to spend time by yourself.

Seriously, did he really just tell me all of this in the first five minutes of a meet and greet? Yes, he did, much to his demise I might add. It was beyond me what some of these guys found appropriate getting-to-know-you conversation. And if he had such a preference for spending time on his own, what was I doing there?

Unlike Secret Agent Man, I did hear from the Mad Scientist again. I was surprised he hadn't noticed how uninterested I was.

No Food Guy

A meet and greet and two dates – two dates that each spanned about six hours – and no food. Did No Food Guy not eat? Did he have some stomach problem that precluded that, or an insecurity about the way he looked when he ate, or a phobia about eating in front of other people? I have no idea which it was, but if I may suggest, don't be No Food Guy. If you are going on a long date, stop for food! The lessons for No Food Guy are the following:

- If you are going to take someone on a long date, let them know to eat before you leave so they don't go hungry or drink on an empty stomach.
- When your date keeps mentioning the restaurants you are passing after four hours of wine tasting, it's probably a hint she'd like to stop for food – take the hint and stop!

There were some lessons for me, too:

- When I'm hungry, I should speak out directly and say, "Hey, No Food Guy, I'm hungry after that hike, let's stop for brunch."

- Rather than worry that a guy isn't stopping for food because he doesn't want to spend more time with me, I should just take care of having my basic needs met.

- If a man continues to take me on long dates without food, he's not the guy for me!

These dates could easily have never happened and my life would be just fine. But I did choose to go on them; no one forced me. At least when I look at them collectively, I can see some important overall lessons.

Valuable lessons learned the hard way

- If communication has red flags up front, stop! Don't proceed to a meet and greet.
- If the meet and greet isn't going well, cut your losses and cut it short.
- People are often clueless on how to interact – we need help!
- Two people on the same meet and greet often have very different perceptions of how the meet and greet went.
- We need to learn to better communicate with each other and learn how to kindly communicate if we would like to continue or stop the interaction.
- We should, above all else, take care of making sure our own basic needs are being met.

CHAPTER TEN

Learning NOT to play with crazy

WHAT IS IT ABOUT ME THAT ATTRACTS THE CRAZIES INTO MY DATING life? I know I lowered my standards for a little while there and met some oddballs, but I'd since been working hard to get the crazy out of my life. I couldn't help but wonder if I'd been going about this all wrong. Because somehow, without knowing how, I suddenly attracted the two most off-the-charts crazy guys of my life.

It's a sad fact of life that there are some pretty unsavory men on these dating sites. Of course, these guys exist in the wild as well. When they pop up on your screen, it can feel as confronting as if they are in person – especially if you've been sucked into the communication already. There's something about having their filthy or degrading words existing on your computer or phone (arguably an extension of yourself) that makes it feel like a big violation. Unfortunately, they may not even be strangers – it's easy to feel a false sense of security if you've met someone in the past, but that doesn't always mean they're a good person or someone you want to have around.

When men like these come along – the ones who are lecherous towards you, derogatory and hateful towards others or, worse, mildly to severely predatory, please, please, please learn from my experiences and run in the opposite direction. After reporting them, of course.

The Big Boob

I'll start this one at the end: I not only blocked the Big Boob, but I also reported him because, in the end, any way you look at it his behavior was inappropriate and abusive.

The Big Boob's messages started out flirty. Almost immediately he asked for my private IM, which I declined – I was always careful not to give out anything that would reveal my last name to someone I didn't yet know. That didn't seem to bother him – in fact, his messages became bolder and progressed from something closer to sexting to mildly inappropriate. He seemed mostly harmless, though, and I was somewhat amused by his overtures.

He became completely preoccupied with finding out one vital piece of information about me: my bra size. Apparently, he "needs a woman of a certain size".

Really? What did that mean and why? I was pretty sure that was a want rather than a need, or was there something missing here? I mean, I know some guys are 'boob guys', but what an odd way to phrase things! He told me he was 35, but my intuition was telling me he might be a bit older. (It wasn't until much later I realized he had actually contacted me a few months prior under a different name, age and profile.)

I didn't particularly want to give him my bra size any more than I wanted to give him my IM, so I just told him I'd tell him when we met. I figured as soon as he saw me he'd be able to figure out if I was the requisite size or not and I would be attracted to him or not and things would go forward … or not. At this point, I was no longer taking any of this seriously or thinking of the Big Boob as anything more substantial than someone to flirt with and short-term entertainment.

When he suggested meeting and gave me ladies' choice on the first date location, I asked if he preferred wine, beer or hard alcohol – you know, to best determine a place to meet. He replied, "I'm a boob and breast man. I want to drink whiskey from your belly button."

Um, not the answer I was looking for or necessarily wanted, but okay. I tried to reel things back in and be more funny than overly suggestive or sexual with, "Then I'd better do a lint check."

That didn't work. He replied, "I bet your lint is lovely and delicious."

What? Yuck! Not sexy. Just strange.

We agreed on a location close to my place but hadn't confirmed the time, so the day of the meet and greet I sent the Big Boob a text: "Hmmm … Haven't heard back from you on a time for tonight so I am guessing you've been kidnapped by a big-breasted woman and are enjoying yourself too much to escape … If you break away let me know."

He apologized profusely, saying his shoot had run over time, and asked if rather than meeting in my neighborhood I'd be willing to drive halfway to meet him. I agreed. As I was getting ready, my phone beeped.

ok … its hot down here as you know … what might you be wearing for me

Something to take advantage of the nice weather ☺

please elaborate a bit im in work hell … give me something to look forward to

Haven't decided what I will be wearing yet. Maybe a dress. What will you be wearing?

a nice dress with no bra …

I made another attempt to steer things back from sexual to funny.

That's what you will be wearing? Hmmm …

I want you to wear your tiniest skirt or dress with no bra

I don't do no bra will wear a pretty bra

can you have your breasts almost spilling out … do you ever wear push up bras … Do you ever go braless out in public

> You ask a lot of questions ... I'll save the answers for when we meet.

> I will pick something nice out to wear I promise! Will do my best not to disappoint

> i dont want nice... i want caliente just have fun with it

I finished getting ready and drove to our halfway point. I messaged to find out where he was, and although he claimed he was there, he refused to tell me where until I disclosed that vital piece of information he had been wanting: my bra size. But I hadn't ever intended on texting that to him.

> im outside ... tell me your bra size and I will come and find you

> Where outside?

I didn't see him anywhere ... I figured he was just playing with me and fully expected he'd pop up in front of me.

answer my question
first please

See for yourself I am standing
out front waiting for you

please tell me first

I'll let you guess are you
even here yet?

im sorry I need the answer first
beautiful yes im here

Not giving you one need to
meet you first

i need your bra size first

Or I could just stand here and text you
until someone comes along and offers to
buy me a drink

your choice ... I need your
bra size first

I'm not going to be pleased if you had me
drive down here to turn and go home

that's not what I want but I
need your true bra size first

I was starting to lose any amusement factor and getting really ticked off.

> 32 aa

haha ... im thirsty ... please tell me what is your size ... that's all it takes

> I'm getting tired of standing here. You seriously going to send me home without meeting me?

I was walking around fuming by now and pretty sure he wasn't actually there.

why so stubborn ... all I need is that one size

> If you were sitting outside here I would see you. I don't think you are here I think you are just messing with me

i not right outside im outside very close by ... i dont like a dominant woman ... tell me your size and I walk right over... i need a woman of a certain size

> I'm a certain size and I'm going home

ok ... so stubborn ... bye

You aren't even here are you?

i ve told you im here ... im very honest

Not so honest. I told you I wouldn't tell you my size before I met you and you agreed to meet me. So why don't we compromise come over here and I will whisper the answer in your ear.

well it told you how important is for me ... I have certain standards

I was fed up and ready for this ordeal to be over one way or another. I had driven an hour to meet him and at least wanted to see what he really looked like, find out who this obnoxious man was before leaving, so I sent my bra size.

i ve compromised enough ... I need a sensual and passionate open minded woman

I just gave you my size. That is what you asked for. And I'm still standing here by myself

> sorry you are not busty enough for me … Your size is only mildly large you would have to have perfect shaped breasts and great nipples for me to be interested

I was exasperated and pissed off, to say the least. I decided to call the Big Boob. He didn't pick up, just sent me another text.

> are you breasts very nice? tell me how sexy they really are … might want to fuck you tonight

The Big Boob then called me, asking more details about my breasts, but I wasn't about to tell him. He asked if they were nice and if I liked him if I would let him suck on them. I told him it was very unlikely at this point that I would like him, and I was leaving. I was so exacerbated I barely even knew what I was saying, but then *he* hung up on *me*.

I was angry. I was upset. My whole body was shaking. And then I realized I had to walk a block to my car. What if he actually had been there watching and was going to jump out and grab me? I anxiously turned the corner and walked to my car … one of the most scary and intense walks of my life. Thankfully, there were enough people milling about that someone would have seen him coming at me.

When I was safely in my car, I felt brave enough to send one last text.

> You are a piece of work

> so are you ... you need to be more straight forward ... I would have fucked you so good I would have had you sucking my big cock off in my car

I didn't reply; I was more than a bit shaky and had an hour drive home.

In hindsight, it's clear I should have just stopped this right at the beginning long before agreeing to meet him, or at the very latest when he started the texts rather than coming over to meet me. I suppose the lure of a sunny Saturday evening – combined with already having driven an hour to meet him – had me reluctant to give up on the prospect of a fun night. I do wonder if the relocation was intentional on his part for this very reason – I like to think that if I'd been closer to home, I'd have put an end to it far sooner. I'd wasted two hours driving, plus 45 minutes standing on the curb texting. What the hell was I thinking? I know I'm smarter than that. Why did I behave that way?

Ugh, I know my mother will probably read this, wonder where she went wrong in raising me and spend the rest of her time worrying more about me than she ever has. I'm generally intelligent and level-headed, and most people who know me will agree with that assessment ... so I have to ask myself what happened here?

The whole thing angers and annoys me, yet I initially felt I had no one to blame but myself for getting into this situation – I should have known better. Or was I just a little naïve? I had really thought this was only a little game of flirting, but by the end of it I was so angry it actually gave me a headache. Had the Big Boob totally manipulated me? Well, clearly he had, but was that his intention from the beginning? Was he even there? Was this how he got off? Was he just angry and wanting to treat women badly or was he actually dangerous?

It seems likely he's a predator of some sort, so when push came to shove, I dodged a bullet or some other form of harm by not meeting the Big Boob. I should probably consider myself lucky it wasn't worse. I'm glad I also reported him because any way you look at it his behavior was inappropriate and abusive. It wasn't until after I had done that that I realized the Big Boob, whoever he may really be, had contacted me under a different profile months before the whole incident.

Jr High Crush

Do you remember your Jr High Crush? Cute, popular and utterly unaware of you? So what happens years later when you get in touch? You may just reunite and find that you were meant to be, and it is the best thing ever that life has brought you back together. Another fairytale that isn't my life. Believe it or not, I quickly learned that my Jr High Crush made the Big Boob almost look sane. As I recount what happened, I can't help but try to figure out why I was even interested in talking to this guy and what we could have possibly had in common. And then I realized, I was a 12-year-old girl, he was a cute, popular boy and I knew absolutely nothing else about him … because when you were 12 that was apparently all that mattered. (Have I actually learned more about how to select a date or a potential partner since then?)

It started out as Facebook friends – he messaged me to ask if I was in touch with his old girlfriend from junior high. Ouch, that hurt! Jr High Crush was still interested in the more popular girl. The 12-year-old in me came out, wondering if these things just never change. Over time, things shifted and he started messaging me more frequently and asked for my phone number so we could text. Before I knew it, he was texting me non-stop, calling me and making plans to come visit. All these years later, did I engage only because the popular guy had finally noticed me?

Just like with the Big Boob, I can't do this level of crazy justice by recounting, so I'll just share the texts. Often he would send multiple texts with no response from me. There is no way I could have made this stuff up, crazy messages, spelling errors and all. Like with the Big Boob, it's hard to say if all of this was more entertaining or disturbing.

> Hmm. According to my laptop... Julie says she's available... however... a kenundrom has emerged... she isn't answering the telephon... hope she's ok.... I may need to call the wambulance... ;-) ? .... ☺

> I was out and about, sorry I missed you.

Can you please call me anytime after 8"40 yout yime pleeeeez... I am killin it at the gym and want to go back...is that ok. I will be up til midnight your time tonight... have to fill out app... break up my monotony and call me tonight pleeez.... ;-) I am looking forward to this one ☺

Ok I will text you first to make sure you are up. Have fun at the gym.

Tx sweetie... I live 2 days like 1 now... should be in Spain or Italy... get up at 6... gym... practice and play by noon..eat TAKE A SESTA..Then go back to gmy and practice till dark..and it rained here... got me a good siesta...lol...don' worry sweetie... I sleep from midnight to 6 to... lol. My waist is 29...same as high school///bit at 150... I bench 225... and am ripped...I think it's a better addiction doncha think...;-)...and tnank you...ttyl. I didn't say that to impress you...but I copmted with the best before at 130 lbs in high school... and now have another 30 pounds of upper body strength...this is gonna be fun....ttyl@

The next day, without a reply from me ...

> I gotta slow down or start proof reading
> my messages to you... I look at them and
> it looks like a 3rd grader write it... sorry..I
> do know how to spel... are there 2 ll's in
> that... ☺... will be up awhile if you have
> timede to chat... let me know what's
> good... lookin forward this one .... Like
> my weekend nights? gym to mysef and
> Dicovery and History channel.... Wow
> times have changed... lol...but belive me...
> I still party....sober ttyl?

We talked on the phone that evening and the phone call was even odder than the text. I spent a lot of time looking a bit cross-eyed at my phone in disbelief about what I had imagined Jr High Crush might be like in reality.

And then the texts started again the next day.

> It was fun talking to you ...
> wow..did we catch up fast...
> and am happy about the way our
> conversation went...and finally
> woman who actually talks into
> the phone too...this is gonna be
> fun... ...and thank you for not
> multitasking when we speak... cuz
> you have MY full attention...nyt
> sweetie... I hope I didn't scare the
> crap out of you... lol@

Good thing he couldn't actually see my multi-tasking or eye rolling.

> I turned the ringer off on my phone so I just realized you texted. It was fun catching up.

It sure was…I'm really looking forward to knowing even more about you…it was very fun to me too…and will be texting you and calling you alot as we get close to meeting…which I can't wait for… this is gonna be a blast…text or call me whenever…can we chat later tonigh again…? I must have liked it…lol You're a nice woman thanks for understanding my situation… mush appreciated…☺ I am getting my thrills out of getting to know you again…your really interesting to me…and the Cinderella stort is less than 2 months away for me after 17 years…I want you to share that with me if your ok with that…?...cuz your super sweet … takin a nap now… you were worth it……☺ You were worth staying up late for…but its sieasta time 4 hours early today for me coz of it…lol

I can probably get you a free plane ticket from a close friend…he's calling me back tommorow after we talk tonight….can you take a week of work?

> Whoever invented the GPS…I would love to kiss their ass…even if it was an 800 pound black woman…its saved my ass over 10000 times….divide that out and he ass is reeeeeal small… no biggy…. and worth it

> Sorry I missed you sweetie… I wa sawing logs…. lol but I have to tell you..it made my day to get yout message…thank you….is it ok with you if I have myself a long-distance crush on you…I think that's what I am having here… hope your sleeping well..it's 4 am there now…but text me when your up and jamming around so we can chat tonight ok you sweet thing….;-)…and thanks again for your message…it's telling me you care…morning joke=did you hear the one about the 2 peanuts walking through L.A….? ..erll…one of them was a salted…………☺…text me cutie when you have time you busy girl… ☺@

Yes, I played the busy card. There was too much texting for me to keep up with and I am not a huge phone person, but talking during my commute was manageable since I had to be in the car anyhow. This was followed by even more texts. He told me what his life had been like and how he had lost all his money to women (that plural is on purpose, not a typo) who he was involved with and were doing his books. And then in the next breath, he asked if I would help him

manage his books. I suggested that perhaps he shouldn't be so trusting
and should consider doing his own books.

Before I knew it, Jr High Crush was planning to come visit me
for a week en route to moving back to our hometown. I have to say I
didn't say no. I was a bit intrigued based on junior high memories and
figured I had nothing to lose. Truth be told, given the stories Jr High
Crush was telling me, I figured there was quite a bit of BS mixed in
with everything he said so I was pretty sure I would never see him.

Morning sexy…I'm looking
forward to seeing you…☺

☺

You make me smile too sweetie..;.I need
that… and I am really looking forward to
seeing you…next week…omg….saweeeeet
☺… break out the Guns and Roses cd and
start playing "home sweet home" for me…
yuou will know how I feel…xoxo And if that
doesn't work for you..pls try Ozzys..'Momma
I'm comin home…ok?....:-)

I am going to bail otta here on Monday so I
have time to spend a couple days with you
sweetie…does that sound ok to you? am
really looking forward to seeing you….when
can we chat sweetie?

> Something very interesting is happening to me when I thinbk about you..............I smile ☺.......see....?..... I can't wait to see you....and go home after 17 years I was beginn8ng to think I may not make it...you better be careful with this mand....I heard he hasn't been with a woman for 11 months....hmmmm..... do you know what that means Miss Julie....lol...?@ It means your even more interesting than ever to me to put it politely......:-)....I'looking forward to chatting with you tonight Jules xoxo..uh ohhhhh..am I in trouble now...?....:-)...no shark biting....pleeeeeeeeezzzzzzz

When we spoke, he asked me for all sorts of advice about his family and I tried to slow him down a bit in terms of his interest in me, explaining that he was just interested because there were no women where he was living. And this is what followed:

> Ohh....your wrong about that one....there are a ton of beautiful women here but I wont let anyone get too close to me because I wont let a woman stop me from getting homl....and they don't have any sharp teeth either.... I have had my opportunities....but I know exactly what I am looking for....and we have a ton in common...I think you are very interesting....and will be very curious to see what kind of chemistry we have.... keep I mind I am a perfect gentleman ....I have never ahd the need o fr desire to force myself upon a woman.... and I have moreclass than todosuch a thing....are you ok with me visiting you with you knowing that ....?

> Of course I am okay with you visiting.

What else was I to say? Although maybe I should have put a stop to it then and there, I was entertained and curious about what would happen. Clearly, I hadn't learned enough of a lesson with the Big Boob.

> Ok good...I was actually neverous there for a minute.....lol.....this is going to be fun...☺.....I have spent my life with high maintenance women who really didn't care about my career....but loved the heck out of themselves....what I was looking for 20 years ago is different than now....big time.... and sweetie please be careful with me cuz I think I am WAY too sensative and emotional for a man... but I cant help it...ok....and pls. keep this between you and I....lol

> I want you to know ....I am so excited I can't sleep..I am sorry to bother you but thought you should know....I have waited a lifetime for this..... and I can't stop thinking about the future....and you too .....xoxo.....:-).....I hope you smile when you wake and read my message sweetie....thanks so much for your help.....:-)

> As I re-read your messages....(something I don't usually do).. I am beginning to realize more and more what a kind and thoughtful woman you are.... And so unselfish....< feel bad cuz all we do is talk about me...I want to know everything about you too ....and having you suggest I rest for my drive is something no woman has ever said to me

before a long road trip…they seemed to only care of themselves…the way you show me you care about me is scoring you more and more points with me…and I liked you to begin with…I am excited about seeing you ….thanks for everything and hipe your having a safe trip…and enjoy time with your loved ones…you deserve it sweetie… and byw…I am very proud of your career….beauty and brains can be lethal…and you know me…I like that #*%!….lol….thanks …saved be a buck there too….good job

The reference to the buck was that he swore so much when we spoke live and acknowledged he needed to work on that – so I said he would have to pay me a dollar for every time he swore.

I was telling a guy friend of mine that I hang out with gay guys because they treat me better than straight guys. The bartender overheard me and said maybe I had been hanging around with the wrong straight guys because there are a lot out there who will treat you well. So maybe you have just been hanging around with the wrong women.

What are you telling me Julie …I know a lot of single women who live in gay communities….are you bi ? ..or gay?

No I am telling you there are a lot of nice women out there who will treat you nicely

A lot of women dont like to be hit on all the time either and live in gay communities bcuz of that too......Kate Moss felt the same way...you scared the crap otta me....it's ok with me as long as your not sleeping with them...geez...I hope not...lol. I know it...i meet them everyday...what are you really saying Julie...you dont think we would be a good match?...we haven't spent quality time together... ever....are you not ready to try and see what it's like together? That's ok with me who your friends are...I want you to be happy and safe...but what kind of man do you want to grow old with...?...

I have no idea! ☺

Why?...your smart...are you Bi?..it wont freak me out ..promise. I am looking for someone I can grow old with I love...what do you want?,,,

No I am not bi. I have no idea why you think that. I just have a better idea of what I don't want than what I do want.

Me too...this is not my first picnic...nor my second...I am very picky who I talk to and see...and your rubbing me toward going home instead of visiting you BASED ON WHAT YOU SAID.....WAAA I was more interested in you...than you were in me obviously... and unless you convince me otherwise...that's how I feel and therefore shouldn't meet you...< dont want to get shark bit....

Jr High Crush called me after without waiting for a response but I was visiting my mom so I wasn't able to really talk. We hung up and he continued texting.

> Lol...ok..but please tell her now that I would like to meet her soon..pleeeeeeeeezzzzzzzzz ☺....xoxo lol. Tell things work out for me ...I promise to buy her a bigger home, assuming her daughter is a good girl...ok?

> I think you should see how things go with me first ;-)

> Deal...xoxo Ok... I wanna ttyl...your more special than you give yourself credit for...I really like you...and trust me... it is nothing to be afraid of...I do my best to spoil my girl...I know....slowwwwww dooooooowwwwwwwnnnnn... lol

> Morning sweetie...I slept like a baby..but didn't dry and crap my pantes last night.... lol....I was at the gym when it opened.. and will be packing ...this is going to be interesting to me....I THINK UOUR WORTH WATING FOR HONEY.........☺

On a phone call while I was driving home, Jr High Crush told me that he smoked cigarettes – this just kept getting better and better for me. Have I mentioned yet that smoking is a deal-breaker for me? I let him know there was no cigarette smoking in my house, and he asked if I was excited to see him. I was trying to be nice when we spoke without giving him false hope or inappropriate encouragement so I told him I would let him know when he arrived. He got upset and I said I was just playing with him. I was just trying to be real.

I wasn't sure where that conversation would leave things. I wasn't sure any conversation would change whether he was really going to be visiting … then the texts continued.

> Ok…you gave me a good reason to quit smoking cigarettes….and I am gonna quit now….but I don't think I will ever quit smoking weed…it helps me sleep…and I have been smoking it since before I met you…I hope that doesn't freak you out but I am honest and I have never meT doctor who said it's a big deal…. there is no proof of causing cancer…and I can spare a few brain cells….we only use less than half of it anyway….I will be waiting for your response on this one…uh ok…lol

He'd be waiting for a while because I wasn't quite sure how to respond to that one. Jr High Crush had told me he'd been sober for a few years and I was trying to calculate how he could be sober for that long if he was smoking pot? This one got stranger and stranger! Even without my reply, of course the texts continued.

> The good news about that is I don't have anything else to hide from you....promise

> Since I am being so honest with you...let me tell you what I think of gays..I think they are sick.. and gay men s lifestyles disgust me big time...I understand they are your friends....but they would never be in my home....ever....or near my friends...cleaning house means to stah away frompeople who wont work for me...and what thehy do makes me sick....I think we need to talk about that more...I can understand you feel safe around them...but I wont have any of those genetic misfits in MY life...and is why God mad Adam and Eve ...not Adam and Steve...

Wow, I so didn't see that one coming! It made me feel sick to my stomach to see something like that written. It left me shaking, so it took me more than a few minutes to have enough composure to even write a response to something so ugly.

Wow those are some pretty strong feelings that I happen to disagree with.

It looks like I am headed straight for home instead of visiting you....gay men have hit on me before....and I am the total opposite of feminine.... let's do eachother a favor before we get hurt...II am making this as easy as possible for us...I wish you thde best with your sick friends Why do you think God invented Aids?... to cleanse the earth...talk to your pastor Mabye is time you read the best selling book ever....the Bible.... read what it says about gays

Those texts came in over a period of hours that afternoon and into the evening. I didn't feel like they deserved a response, so I didn't reply to any of them. I felt as sick to my stomach as I did when dealing with the Big Boob. It's amazing what an impact a text can have on a person. I had thought since the beginning it was unlikely Jr High Crush would make it to visit. While it was no skin off my back that he wasn't coming to visit, this whole last exchange really bothered me. It deeply saddens me that there are people out there who think like that and that I had been conversing with one of them.

Early morning another text came in ...

> It sucks being so emotional....I fell sad because I told you ...your hanging out with gays is no big deal to me when it actuallybis...there is NO WAY I could return home....and have gay people around me...my reputation would be at stake....and I don't approve of their lifestyles...it's sad it's a deal-breaker for us.... but do hope we can remain friends and you figure out what your looking for and what you want in life...I am sorry and will really miss seeing you.

I didn't respond to that or future messages he sent to me over Facebook. I will forever be oh-so-thankful he didn't have my home address! I can only imagine what a disaster that visit would have been if we had got to the point of meeting in person, or what he might have done if he knew my address. I got lucky on that one too. Hopefully, lesson learned on dealing with the crazies and *please* let me stop attracting this into my life! Such a waste of time and energy.

CHAPTER ELEVEN

Testing out being proactive

FOOL ME ONCE, SHAME ON YOU; FOOL ME TWICE, SHAME ON ME. YES, shame on me. Time has always been a precious commodity to me, so what was I doing wasting it on crazies? I needed to be a bit more selective and cut loose the guys who weren't appropriate to date. I deserved better than that, and if I was going to attract better men, I needed to stop wasting my time on interactions that served no purpose.

That was all good in theory, but after a string of communications that didn't even lead to a meet and greet, and meet and greets that didn't even lead to a date, I was growing weary. Some of them came close at times and I would get my hopes up. So many people said it was a numbers game. If that's true, I would hate to see how much time and effort it would take to get the numbers in my favor to find a good meet and greet that could turn into more. I didn't like the odds with these numbers, and for me, this wasn't a game, it was my life. So ixnay on the idea of this being a numbers game. I needed less numbers and more quality.

As I worked on culling down the field to more appropriate candidates, it was tempting to go back and match with more guys so I could have more interactions to choose from. As I got more selective, I realized I was missing the daily onslaught of messages. I had gotten used to them and was having withdrawals from the attention. While a lot of the messages were annoying, the sweet ones, even if they weren't from men I would want to meet, certainly felt good. My thoughts and emotions about all of this were up and down with the week, depending on who was contacting me and what they were saying. I hate to admit how much I allowed this to affect my moods and emotions. Looking back, I see it clearly, but I'm not sure I fully understood the extent of the impact at the time.

While some of it had been so outrageous I found it amusing, and although I was continuing to learn some things, it wasn't enough to account for the time spent. Even if I needed to adjust to fewer flattering messages and dopamine hits from my phone constantly beeping with new messages, I was ready to find someone who could hold my interest for more than a meet and greet and who was interested in me as well. For what, you ask? Truth be told, I still wasn't sure; I just knew I wanted to spend some time with someone whose company I enjoyed. Maybe it was time to take matters into my own hands and see what happened.

Ladies' Choice

It's my theory that, overall, the guys like to do the selecting and chasing. I'm actually mostly okay with that – I guess I'm a little old-fashioned that way, too. I would much rather be pursued than do the pursuing. Do I lose my feminist card again? But, since I wasn't having a lot of luck with waiting to be selected, I took the initiative and reached out to Ladies' Choice. I think I only did this around three times, and out of the three, Ladies' Choice was the only one I met.

What made me reach out to Ladies' Choice? His profile was witty and his picture was cute. He was a few years older than me, but not too many, and I'll mention yet again how much I appreciate wit. At the time, I was blissfully unaware Ladies' Choice had poached his witty statement from somewhere else. Not in and of itself a bad thing – if you reference where you took it from, then at least I know you are well-read. If you don't reference then, well … I don't want to have to suggest plagiarism, but ...

I seem to keep learning things the hard way, and the evening of our meet and greet I learned that a profile with just one photo (with sunglasses, no less) probably wasn't enough to tell what a guy looked like. Ladies' Choice looked nothing like his photo, but I quickly forgot about that when the bouncer at the bar he selected carded me on the way in. That was a bit of an ego boost! The meet and greet was starting to look up … and we hadn't even gotten to know each other yet.

It took a nosedive again once we were seated at the bar. Ladies' Choice wasn't very talkative and it was like I was pulling teeth to get him to actively participate in the conversation. I'm not sure if that was because he was uninterested, nervous, shy and/or sober but after a while he warmed up and got more chatty. Once again this was a situation with drinks and no dinner, so I felt I was doing pretty well, all things considered. I think the adrenaline of meeting someone new helps with that somehow, though I can't say why. I love my food and it is especially helpful when I've been drinking.

Or maybe I wasn't handling it was well as I thought. We left the second bar and the next thing I knew we were making out ... in public ... on the street. Weren't we too old for that? At least the kids in line didn't scream out, "Get a room, grandma and grandpa!" That would have been humiliating. Ladies' Choice was clearly okay with it all because before ending the evening he asked for a date.

The next few days were filled with a combination of witty texts that clearly weren't plagiarized and some behaviors that seemed a little odd. That didn't stop me from seeing Ladies' Choice again, but I filed that insight away. My age-old question – was I missing or ignoring signs I should have been paying attention to that were telling me this was the wrong guy? – reappeared, which was in conflict with the thought that maybe I should just have fun with someone until a point where I was no longer having fun or didn't like how I was being treated and reassess at that point. What was the right way to handle these things and figure them out? Or at least the smart way to maximize the fun and minimize the heartache?

Another night, another bar and Ladies' Choice was sporting some really tight jeans. Deal-breaker? Hmmm ... we would have to see. He was in really good shape, so that wasn't the problem; it was more just a question of style (or lack of). This time we had some bar snacks to go with our drinks – yay! A much better idea for me than drinks on an empty stomach. And conversation flowed right from the start, so maybe this could go somewhere. It was getting late and Ladies' Choice suggested we walk to his place so he could pick up his car and give me a ride home – I think I've heard this line before ;-)

As we headed up to his place to get his keys Ladies' Choice kissed me in the elevator (more somewhat public kissing, but he was a good kisser), but left me in the hall while he went inside to grab said keys. Maybe it wasn't so much of a line after all. Was his place a mess and he didn't want me to see it? Did he not really like me that much? Or maybe he sensed I was a bit uneasy or thought it was too soon to invite me in? Whatever it was, I was a bit relieved. I still wasn't sure what was right or wrong at this stage. My need for an etiquette guide or set of rules for such matters wasn't going away.

I teetered between feeling it was okay to just go for it and have fun, and *OMG what kind of sleaze have I become?* There had to be a happy medium in there somewhere. I knew that in the end it was my decision to make for myself and that decision might be different with different people and situations. But whatever that decision turned out to be, I needed to be sure I was comfortable with it and okay with what the consequences, if any, might be.

So far it seemed I was willing to move faster with someone I wasn't interested in than someone I was, because if it turned out to be just sex with someone I didn't foresee any possibility of a future with, then there was nothing to lose. Sometimes I think this makes sense; other times I think it doesn't. Have the rules changed for this? Or maybe I am just changing. Or maybe I shouldn't have any rules? Seems I might be just as confused now as ever. I'm not sure I was capable of digging deep for the answers to these questions in that moment. Maybe that was okay. Maybe it was just supposed to be a process of exploration and trial and error, not set rules.

I love convertibles and Ladies' Choice had a very nice one, but it was a brand (which shall remain nameless) that from my experience mostly assholes drive. Maybe I shouldn't stereotype by car brand? Or maybe I should ... time would tell. This time there was no discussion of another date or any stated indication he would contact me again, so as I got out of the car, I was prepared not to hear from him. I was constantly looking for patterns or clues to these sorts of things, but I am not at all sure guys think about behaving consistently so a woman can figure out what to expect. Who knows?! Certainly not me at that point in time.

Two nights later, the phone rang. He was going away for the weekend, so he was just calling to talk rather than to set another date. I wasn't used to this! I hadn't gotten to a point with any guys where they called just to talk. Up to this point, calls were only placed to make plans and most plans were actually made via text. It felt a little odd to have a guy calling just to talk. But this was a nice odd for a change.

I asked Ladies' Choice where he was staying for the weekend, meaning which town. He replied, "With some friends," and it sounded as if I'd caught him off guard. Funny – I was just making conversation and curious where he was traveling to, not trying to find out who he was seeing. It wasn't my business; we weren't exclusive. Judging by his response, though, it was likely female and quite possibly a date. I know I referred to my other dates as having dinner, drinks or whatever it might be with a 'friend'. I think that was totally fair and appropriate at such an early stage. I've not figured out any other way to handle conversations like that when non-exclusive dating is going on. We were, after all, all participating in online dating, so we all had to know there were other meet and greets and dates taking place; there was just no need to rub it in anyone's face. I may sound like a broken record, but I have to ask yet again, where is the book of rules with all the proper dating etiquette?

The next few dates didn't end just at the hallway. We planned our first real 'dinner' date for an actual full meal at a restaurant, but we started that off with a glass of wine at my place, ended up drinking and talking and (let your imagination go) we never made it to dinner. Which was just fine. As much as I love my food, I could have dinner any night – fun sexual encounters were not as frequently on the menu. He didn't stay the night, nor did I when we ended dates at his place. And that was just fine too.

What wasn't fine was the call from Ladies' Choice the following Monday at 10:35 pm. To start with, that was a little late to be calling. He was very distant and he didn't seem to have anything to say. So why was he calling? Was he a bit drunk? Hard to say for sure. I couldn't understand why he was calling and then staying silent so I started to talk, and he spoke up at the same time, finally spitting out: "I have been dreading having this conversation. I've been seeing someone else and I think I've complicated things."

"Okay," I replied, stifling a bit of a laugh. Have I mentioned I tend to respond to tense or uncomfortable situations with a bit of involuntary laughter? Not belly laughing, more like "hmph" sounds or a bit of nervous laughter. That was followed by what seemed like another very long silence, which I broke with, "I am not quite sure what you want me to say." I could only take these empty silences for so long. Here was a man whose profession required him to speak for a living, so one would think he'd be better at this.

After more silence he continued. "I don't know, I feel really bad." Silence, again.

"Really, I don't know what you want me to say ... Good luck with her? Thanks?"

Silence. Then, "I was really dreading this. I feel bad."

"Well, you should." The tone of my voice was a combination of disbelief and uncertainty about whether I should be hurt or insulted or just think it was all funny. The extracurricular activities were fun with Ladies' Choice, but outside of that, something just felt off – maybe even a bit boring. I'm not sure it could have ever evolved to something more than sex.

After more silence and more of me saying I wasn't sure what he'd wanted me to say, I finally just said, "Well, bye" and he said, "bye". And that was it.

But really, what the hell was that? On the bright side, at least he didn't just disappear or send a text. See what an optimist I am? I can find the bright side in anything.

I wasn't *too* bothered by the whole ordeal, but part of me thought maybe I'd let him off too easy. Or maybe not. Should I have said something else? Should I have followed up that conversation with a text saying, "Just curious, was going out to dinner just a ruse and in actuality you were just swinging by to tell me you didn't want to see me anymore, and then accidentally slept with me and forgot to tell me you couldn't see me anymore because you were seeing someone else?"

On top of that, it felt like a bit of a formal break-up for not really having anything to break up. We had never said anything about exclusivity, and I had assumed he was seeing other people. Maybe he didn't realize I was doing that too? Funnily enough, the other guy I was seeing at the time seemed to want to go in the direction of not seeing other people and I was fretting over that and trying to figure out what to do. So, in all actuality, the timing of Ladies' Choice's call made life much easier for me. But being 'dumped' once again made me question myself and my value rather than questioning him. Why was that? Was it human nature? Would I be able to fix that in myself? I'd like to. I knew it wasn't a good idea to let others influence my self-worth.

I talked to a friend to get some perspective. She thought maybe he had been calling to clear his conscience and wasn't telling me it was over. I thought she was way off base. She said she didn't think that would be the last of him, and that my response or lack thereof probably left him wondering if I was ever really interested in him. I didn't seem to be getting any better at giving or receiving appropriate cues or communication.

Maybe I was right to stereotype based on the brand of Ladies' Choice's car?

CHAPTER TWELVE

Congratulations, it's a relationship

WHILE ALL OF THAT HAD BEEN GOING ON WITH LADIES' CHOICE, there was another man in the background who sought me out and had a much better plan of pursuit from the get-go. Maybe there really was something to letting them make the first move. Or does that thought process play into a power dynamic I don't really want to play into? I had one of the guys I met tell me about a book he had read to help him become a good dater and find the right partner. Even though it was written for men, I read it thinking it might have some insight for me and my clients on both sides of the equation. I was horrified that this bestselling author had turned dating into a game with rules only the reader of the book knew about. The most offensive rule was a man should test out how well his date would follow him... not just on the dance floor but in life in general. The guy who suggested this book insisted this was a good way to find a *partner* and didn't seem to comprehend finding someone to follow you wouldn't be creating a *partnership*. I had higher hopes than that for Tour Guide ... but looking back, perhaps he had read the same book and was just smoother at executing. I wonder if things would have been different if I had read that book back then and knew what I know now ...

A good meet and greet; an even better first date

It started with some messages back and forth over a couple of weeks because I was busy and stacking up (or should I say backing up) the dates with a few others. The first message he sent started with a subject line that was in response to my profile headline and said, "Many, many nice qualities ..." so he seemed witty and wasn't starting with any plagiarism. He was clearly eager to meet me, as his reply to my proposed date was, "I am hoping to meet you sooner than that." He preferred email over texting, which seemed odd, but I later learned that was because he had a flip phone, not a smartphone ... which seemed even odder. He was the only person I had come across who worked in technology and didn't have a smartphone. Strange? Quirky?

Rather than a typical meet and greet, Tour Guide planned a full-blown date including an hour-long drive to a spot he said had the best oysters around. This could obviously get to be a very long drive if things didn't go well. I may not have been completely sold on him but the phrase "best oysters ever" definitely won me over. Yum! At the very least there would be a new culinary discovery.

The morning of the oyster quest, I woke up to a text from Tour Guide wanting to move our start time, and then another a bit later asking if I would drive five minutes away from my place to meet him so he didn't have to drive as far. Ugh, he showed so much promise with his planning ... was he now going to turn into a flake? <sigh> This wasn't making me happy or excited to meet him; it was just all a bit aggravating. It got worse. Next, I got a message letting me know that because it was sunny I might end up driving us back because he didn't do so well in the sun and might get sunstroke or feel a little 'pukey' ... more interest points deducted for this. Yet, there was still something that kept me going. Was it learning about where to find the best BBQ oysters? Or was I actually drawn to this guy for some reason?

I figured the best thing for me to do was try to keep him feeling well so I stopped by the store and bought some bottles of water and some sunscreen. Tour Guide pulled up in a convertible (not the asshole brand) with the top down ... fun for a drive on a nice day, but what about the sunstroke?

He got out of the car to greet me and I saw he was wearing a baseball cap, sunglasses, T-shirt with a loose grey hoody over it, cargo shorts and tennis shoes with white socks. It wasn't too-tight jeans, but it wasn't much better. Add interest points for convertible and then deduct for attire.

As he hugged me hello, he asked, "Do you have cash on you?" I was a bit shocked both by the remark and by my realization that, oh crap, no I didn't! I had meant to get some cash when I picked up the water and sunscreen and forgot that! I didn't think Tour Guide needed to know that before I had even met him, I had done everything necessary to take care of him for the day and had forgotten to take care of the cash for myself. (Yes, this was a recurring theme and something he and other people have made me more and more aware of. I'd been trying, clearly not successfully enough, to remedy this.) While that was going on in my mind, I simply answered, "No, I don't, do I need some?"

In his thick foreign accent he said, "Girly, you are going to get into a car with a complete stranger and drive for over an hour away from your home with him with no cash on you in case something happens and you need to get away or said stranger leaves you on the side of the road?" Add back major interest points; this guy was funny.

The chitchat flowed easily and he seemed quite the gentleman, telling me that if I was afraid of his fast driving he'd slow down because he didn't want to make me uncomfortable … but also, not to worry because he was very fond of his own ass and wasn't about to take chances that would put it in harm's way. (I didn't yet know this was part of a conversation he was weaving in throughout the day to prepare me for the following evening … but I did put it all together after our second date … well, technically first, since this was a meet and greet even if it was more date-like.)

As promised, the oysters were delicious. We both enjoyed the food, drink and company immensely. His gentlemanly ways continued with opening my car door, leaving me at the table to get comfortable while he ordered, paying for the meal and talking about his parents in an endearing manner. On the drive home, Tour Guide asked if I was free the following evening. Clearly a successful meet and greet! I was non-committal at first, but he said it was a surprise that involved the full moon and I'd just need to be at his place by 8:30 pm and I'd be home by 10 pm to get plenty of sleep before my early meetings the following day.

Hmmm, interesting. That meant, with travel time, a one-hour date – not much time together, but okay, I like a good surprise. I was guessing Tour Guide had some special place to go see the full moon and was probably bringing along a picnic and champagne or something. I wasn't so sure how that would be a surprise, but okay, whatever floated his boat. For some reason I couldn't quite fathom, I continued to be intrigued by this man. Probably his passion and his planning and his mysterious date ... what the heck, I'd bite.

I arrived at 8:30 pm on the dot. As we were getting in the car to go for his 'surprise', I noticed Tour Guide had a safety pin attached to the breast of his shirt. Was part of the intrigue how odd he was? Oh well, maybe it was a key to a locked gate that would give us entrance to a private beach or something to sit and watch the moon?

As we drove, Tour Guide started to tell me that we were going to go look at the moon from up high. There goes the beach idea. I was a bit stumped.

Me: "Are you taking me on a helicopter ride?"

Tour Guide: "No, a plane ride."

"Are you flying the plane?"

"Yes."

(In my head) *Okay, Julie, breathe ...*

I was excited, interested and even more intrigued, and also wondering if I should be trusting this guy with my life. Rewind to the day before and his conversation about driving, keeping his own butt safe and, oh yes, the casual question about whether I had ever been in a small plane before. Ding, ding, ding! Tour Guide was an evil genius (it seemed in a good way at this moment) and master planner. He had been setting the stage for this moment since just a few minutes after we met. Impressive!

Me: "So how long have you been flying?"

Tour Guide: "Three weeks."

"So we are going up with your instructor?"

"No, just me."

(Heart pounding out of my chest.) "Wait, I don't know much about this stuff, admittedly, but I am pretty sure if you have been flying for just three weeks, they wouldn't let you take a plane up at night by yourself."

"Who said they're LETTING me take it?"

Okay, think quick, what is going on here? "Okay, you're pulling my leg – really, how long have you been flying?"

"Three weeks."

"Come on, seriously."

"Three weeks."

"Come on, this isn't something to joke about, are you pulling my leg?"

"Girly, I can keep this up for a long time."

A bit more banter and then …

"And you never ask a pilot how long they have been flying – that is irrelevant. You ask how many hours they have."

We finally came to an understanding that Tour Guide had a few years and plenty of hours under his belt (which may have actually added up to three weeks' worth of hours of flight time) and no one was *letting* him take the plane because it was his plane. Exasperating! And yet, more intriguing than ever.

Fortunately, Tour Guide seemed quite safe and diligent about the pre-flight check while I stood there debating with myself if I was stupid or adventurous for getting in a small plane with someone I had met a little over 24 hours ago. What the hell! I was going for it. Again, I just had a feeling about this guy and sensed it would all be okay. That didn't mean my heart wasn't continuing to pound outside of my chest!

I was seated in the plane adjusting my seatbelt when he said, "Can you please spread your legs so I can put my hand between them." I'm sure there wasn't any other way to get my seat adjusted. The guy was funny, I'd give him that. And then Tour Guide explained to me that it was Federal Aviation Administration (FAA) regulation to "kiss the pilot" before taking off. Smooth! How many times had he used those lines? I hadn't pegged him as a player, but ...?

I looked at him and laughed and thought to myself that I really didn't want to kiss him because while I liked his personality, I wasn't at all sure I was attracted to him – and at that moment he kind of had bad breath. While I was busy thinking, he leaned over and kissed me and then shut my door. Pilot kissed; FAA regulations apparently met.

Take-off was a bit nerve-racking – not because of his skill, just because WTF was I doing?! But ... oh my God, it was amazing! The view was breathtaking.

I don't think the moon has ever been so beautiful. I just kept looking around in awe. I reached for my purse to take a picture and Tour Guide threw it out of reach saying, "You can take pictures next time ... this way I can make sure you come back with me again." Oh, the smooth continued. The whole thing was exhilarating and there was definitely something sexy about watching Tour Guide take control and fly!

He landed perfectly and we drove back to his place to get my car. As I came out of his bathroom, Tour Guide looked at me and laughed.

Me: "What, why are you laughing at me?"

Tour Guide: "I was just thinking how lucky you are that I like you."

"Excuse me, why does that make me lucky?"

"Well you have told me a couple of stories of things that have happened to you with your dating, stories that you hear about or see on TV, not in real life, and I figure there is one story missing. The one where the girl comes out of the bathroom and the guy is lying naked on the sofa. So, you are really lucky I like you and want to see you again, or else you would have come out and found me lying naked on the sofa with a rose between my teeth."

Okay, this guy was super funny and witty too, and he just took me flying to see the full moon on our first date. Checkmate?

I followed up with an email: "Thanks so much for the surprise. It was really spectacular. That takes sweeping a girl off her feet to a whole new level."

He replied, "Thank you for (yet again) trusting a somewhat (by now) stranger with crazy ideas with your life (literally both times). Every time you agree with me without asking too many questions and then when it is obviously a little unsettling you still go with me. It makes me thankful for the profile you have written and the inspiration I have had to write to you. That was a literal sweep. I guess it gives a whole new meaning to having your feet up in the air … However, the level was not that high, come with me again and we can talk about a new level ☺. I hope you got some sleep. I am (somewhat, because I cannot be but a little selfish and happy you agreed to see me) sorry it took a little longer than anticipated. But the moon comes out when she wants, and all a boy can do is wait ☺."

Charming in person, charming in email. Now the trick was to be able to separate the date from the guy and make sure I liked the guy as much as the date.

"Girlfriend material"

The meet and greet and first date with Tour Guide were clearly the most successful throughout this process to date … and possibly the best ever in my lifetime. (Although, I am fortunate to have had some other really amazing first dates, all before online dating, which makes me wonder how much online dating has changed this sort of thing and has it changed it forever?) I mean, how many girls get taken flying as a surprise on a first date? The question really should be, how many girls were considering themselves lucky because Tour Guide had taken them on that date? I needed to figure out if I liked this guy, but I also needed to figure out if this was something special or his standard routine.

When asked, Tour Guide told me plane rides were only reserved for special people, not something he does all the time, and he would only take up a woman who is "girlfriend material". While that could have made me feel special, instead it left me wondering how he knew

I was "girlfriend material" from what seemed like the beginning of the first meet and greet. And what was the likelihood of him telling me, "Yeah, I do this all the time and it always works," if that really was the case?

Truth be told, I wasn't worrying *too* much because I'd also been out with Ladies' Choice and still had other guys contacting me. So even though the first date with Tour Guide brought me to new levels in the atmosphere, I still had my feet well-grounded and was definitely not putting all my eggs in his basket.

I wasn't yet ready to declare Tour Guide a winner, but I liked him. There was a lot of mental chemistry, but I wasn't sure if there was enough physical chemistry – and the physical interactions started out a little rocky, which didn't help matters. It was enough for me to continue to see him and see what might evolve, but for him, we were not seeing enough of each other. I didn't think telling him that was because my dating dance card was full would win me any points, so I told him I was giving all that I could and wasn't ready to have this conversation.

How *could* I have that conversation with him anyhow? I hadn't even had it with myself. All this time I had only thought about meeting someone I enjoyed spending time with. I'd never stopped to think what would happen when I met someone I liked. And I wasn't sure I was even ready to explore that on my own, let alone discuss it with a date. Meanwhile, Tour Guide continued racking up the bonus points. He did sweet things like offering to bring me lunch on a busy day at the office, planning excellent dates and always making another plan to see me before leaving a date.

I felt cared for and appreciated and that felt good. At the same time, I could see he was also still on the dating site daily. I didn't know if he was dating, wooing, shopping or just looking ... and I was doing all of those things myself and going out on other dates, so I couldn't really complain. But it bothered me to see him doing it. I continued to ask myself if I would like him as much if our first date wasn't a plane ride? I couldn't answer that question any more than I could know if I was special or just one of many who was taken on that plane ride.

𝒮

THINGS SEEMED TO BE MOVING ALONG WELL. AND THEN IT HAPPENED ...

No, I didn't fall head over heels and drop the other guys. I did, however, get them confused. I brought Tour Guide out with friends for the first time, not because I was ready to take that step, but because I had errantly double-booked and needed to combine events. That was the first error.

The second happened when my friends mentioned that the U2 concert they had tickets for had been canceled and I turned to Tour Guide and said, "Same as you".

He looked at me funny and said, "Not me, must be the other guy."

"Oh, no," I responded, "now I remember I was talking about it at lunch yesterday with one of my co-workers." Meanwhile, I was hoping I was not bright red because Tour Guide was actually right. It was Ladies' Choice who had told me about that on our date the night before. Note to self: do not confuse Tour Guide with Ladies' Choice, or any of the others for that matter.

The next meeting with Tour Guide and my friends was on purpose, not a scheduling mishap. After the Gay Boyfriends spent a night out with us, they told me they loved him! Which annoyed me a little bit because I, myself, wasn't yet completely sold. Part of what my friends liked was how he treated me and how he seemed head over heels for me. He charmed them the way he was charming me. And the physical interactions were greatly improved after the almost no-go start. Who wouldn't be a little smitten by a message saying, "When I see you on Sat I am going to check every inch of your body to make sure you are a woman. You are gorgeous and I am interested in you, you could make me do anything you want me to."

The girlfriend, then NOT the girlfriend

The relationship just kind of happened; I hadn't planned for it or expected it. Tour Guide became the frontrunner and the other guys magically faded away. I had been doing this dating thing for six months and never once given a thought to what would happen when I met a guy I liked. With so much time spent dating, I never really made time to stop, think and really process … everything just *happened.*

Out shopping one day, Tour Guide said to the sales guy, "It's not for me, it's for my girlfriend." I almost choked. What did that mean? Why was he saying that? Was I ready to be that? I was uncomfortable hearing myself called that, but why? Lots of questions, no answers – a seemingly common theme in my dating life. I still had other guys contacting me. Admittedly, I liked the outside attention, but I wasn't looking to date anyone else … yet I wasn't ready to completely settle in with Tour Guide. Or so I thought.

Before I even realized it, we had been together almost a year. I had literally fallen into a relationship without giving any thought to it. My life seemed in balance, though, and I was enjoying myself, so why give it more thought?

And then we had our first serious fight. It went on and off all day, and into the evening out to dinner with friends. Not that they could tell; I had years of practice at making it seem like everything was okay. It heated up when we were alone and in bed at my place and Tour Guide got out of bed and said, "Fine, I'll just leave."

I'm not sure if I started to cry before or after that (no, not like me to cry, it was likely the drinks I'd had) but I said I didn't want him to leave because, "I wasn't ready for it to be over *yet*." Did he catch the "yet"? Did that change everything? Did I really mean to say "yet"? Was that the alcohol or a Freudian slip? I'm pretty sure now it was just the honest truth slipping out. And he may have known that because while he stayed, things were never the same after that.

Slowly, over the next few months, Tour Guide become moody and a bit of a pill. He went on a three-week business trip and I just had a feeling he was going to come back and dump me. I started feeling anxious, but my friends reassured me, "Tour Guide is totally in love with you, we can see he adores you." The night before his return, I talked to Boy Friend and he told me it was all in my head and I was acting *crazy*. Was he right?

Tour Guide was arriving close to midnight and didn't want me to pick him up. That could mean "I don't want to see you" or "I am getting off a really long flight late at night and just want to go home after being gone for three weeks." It could go either way; I wasn't sure. When I asked if there was anything special he wanted to do the next day, his reply was, "I just want to hang out, just seeing you will be special." Yes, no, mixed messages?

In the morning, when Tour Guide arrived at my door, I went to kiss him hello and he kind of brushed away. He then sat on a chair across the room, and I patted the sofa next to me and said, "What are you doing, come sit over here." In that moment I knew I was not *crazy*, I was *right*.

Things just weren't progressing for him and he didn't see a future (he'd said that when we first started dating about me ... had the tables turned now?). I got a bit defensive; I couldn't help it, I was hurt. "Sure, this is easy for you, you get to come over here and dump me and walk away and you are done. Me, I incorporated you into my life, now I have to go and explain to my friends who've all met you that you dumped me. I've learned a good lesson; I won't do that again."

And then when I asked if this meant we were over, Tour Guide replied he hadn't really thought about it, "But yeah, I guess we are done." How the hell had he not really thought about that part? Had he been looking for me to declare my love for him and when I just got defensive and mad instead of sad, he backed off and was done?

Tour Guide walked out the door and I picked up the phone and called Boy Friend. He answered with "Hello", to which I replied, "Don't ever call me *crazy* again!"

I made myself busy the rest of the day, made plans for the rest of the week and set up dinner on Valentine's Day with one of the Gay

Boyfriends. I was damned if I was going to let Tour Guide get me down. Just take action, fill up your time, don't stop to process or be sad. It seems I went into this mode automatically, naturally, without thinking … I was going out of the relationship the same way I'd gone into it.

The sadness I wouldn't let myself feel quickly turned to anger. I started wondering, *Did he really treat me as well as I thought, or did I just have my rose-colored glasses on again?* Upon reflection, I started to see that while Tour Guide always planned great things to do, they were always things *he* wanted to do – he never asked me what *I* wanted. He was just so good at planning dates, I didn't notice.

The thing that worried me most was not that he was gone, but what if once again I'd been so blinded by the good that I hadn't seen the bad? If the bad really was there, then I hadn't actually learned to pick a better mate. Which meant I wasn't any further along than when all this dating first started. I wasn't sure how to figure out what was real and what wasn't.

Debriefing and undumping

Tour Guide said from the beginning that he didn't stay in touch with exes. When it's over, it's over – he didn't go back, and he didn't stay in touch. So there was no doubt in my mind it was over for good. But I realized I had questions I wanted answered, and I was hell-bent on learning from this experience. It was time to put myself first and think about what I wanted.

I sent Tour Guide an email asking if he would be willing to get together and talk, because while he had been thinking about this for at least three weeks, it was sudden for me and I hadn't had time to process things. I wanted some answers. The subject line of the email read "A favor please" or something to that effect. I knew that even if Tour Guide *wasn't* the good guy I thought he was, he wanted to feel like the good guy and would respond by doing me a favor. I was right; he agreed to come over.

Discussing relationship 'stuff' wasn't my strong point, so I hatched a plan to make the discussion into a focus group of sorts, which added a little humor and removed a bit of anxiety.

And so I began, "Thank you for coming to my focus group. I want to remind you that the people in the back room are just there to observe. Ha-ha. You should not tailor your answers to what you think they would like to hear, but rather answer the questions honestly."

Tour Guide chuckled and said, "Wait a minute, you forgot to say that if at any time I am uncomfortable, I am welcome to leave and I will still receive the full stipend."

To which I replied, "Oh, I didn't forget, you are not welcome to leave before I am done *and* there will be no stipend." I thought I was very funny … I think he did too, even though it made him squirm.

Questions, questions, questions. The answers were mostly satisfying. No, there wasn't anyone else. No, he wasn't ending this to start something new. And some not as satisfying … No, he couldn't explain what he was feeling or why he didn't see a future; he just didn't. At the end of our conversation, I felt proud of myself for putting myself out there to ask the questions and stand up for myself. It felt like we communicated more openly than we ever had – what is it in human nature that doesn't allow us to do that until after a relationship has ended?

At that moment I felt good – perhaps that was because I hadn't yet seen or processed that although he seemed like a good guy because there wasn't *something* making him dump me, he'd still given me no concrete answers to why he didn't want to be with me. His answers weren't complete; the mixed messages had actually continued. I don't think that was on purpose – I think it was because he was in conflict himself.

I woke up the next morning to a *very* unexpected email from Tour Guide saying that neither of us really asked how the other was feeling *now* and some more musings about things. Was he opening the door back up? I wrote back, gently pointing out that while he hadn't actually expressed how he felt in that email, I would put myself out there *again* and say if he wanted to ask me out again, I would definitely say yes. To which he replied, without sharing how he was feeling, he was free the following night if I wanted to talk some more. Seriously? WTF?

Did Tour Guide know how to do anything other than send me mixed messages? I mean, let's go back to the "just seeing you will be special" message. Having him come over and dump me didn't feel very special … I know he was born and raised in another country, but I can't imagine that was categorized as special anywhere on this planet, or the universe for that matter!

Still, I agreed to have him come for a talk. After a couple of hours of talking, we decided to take a walk over to the park to see if we could see the full moon (yes, it all comes full circle). We couldn't see her, but we played on the swings like we were kids. The whole thing was a little awkward and then Tour Guide grabbed me and kissed me. I mean, full make-out session in the park with a man who was usually anti-PDA. I was shocked. And not really feeling it … most likely because my defenses were still up. I was protecting myself from being hurt again. Even so, we went back to my place and sealed the deal. He didn't stay the night, but before he left he was making plans to see me again and checking my availability for Valentine's Day. So, we are back together??? That hadn't been part of the discussion. Nothing in our discussion pointed to anything about us continuing to see each other … and yet we did.

Limbo land

It had been a few months and things were *seemingly* back on track. I was comfortable enough to say, "Remember when we were talking and agreed we needed to continue to have conversations about what is going on? I wanted to check in and see where we are." I didn't like the answer. Tour Guide explained that nothing had really changed, things still didn't feel like they were progressing, but rather that we were just friends with benefits. Hmmm … and ouch! That wasn't what it was seeming like to me. So, not actually back on track.

I guess his definition of friends with benefits was different than mine, because my definition didn't include spending the entire weekend together or coming over to sit on my sofa and hang out and rub my back all day when I was sick. It stung to hear that, but based on how he treated me, I just didn't believe it. His words and actions were saying two different things. The mixed messages continued. Yet, no matter what Tour Guide said, I still wanted to be with him ... not because I was a masochist (at least, that's what I tell myself) but because I really enjoyed our time together and all in all he was very good to me. While he said he didn't love me, he was far better to me and I felt far better about our 'relationship' than those with other men who'd told me they loved me, so I was good. Or so I thought. Was I fooling myself?

Another check-in provided me with this gem: "I'm just not in love with you. I really like you and enjoy your company, but I don't love you, so I feel like I'm not being fair to you." Ouch. That stung even more. And it didn't help that he couldn't articulate what was missing or what else he would want. I felt loved and adored and cared for, so for me, that was all that mattered. I had never felt so supported by someone who cheered me on when things were going well at work, threatened to beat up my boss or co-workers if I complained they were not treating me right, came to me for career advice and discussions and consultations, and so on. I always felt Tour Guide was completely on my side and I was completely on his and that supportive feeling was wonderful. Between his actions and his words, more mixed messages ... or was I missing something? Everyone I knew, including *experts*, agreed: mixed messages. I was not crazy ... or at least, not about this topic.

Slowly it started to feel like he was slipping away. He wasn't quite as interested, there were no more plans made in advance and I'd have to ask if we were getting together rather than just taking it as a given. It was time for another talk.

"I don't love you and I don't see a future with you. I can't see more than a month or two out. I don't know that we will be together in a year, so I feel like I am not being fair to you and I am being selfish."

These talks never seemed to bring me joy. Yet, I still didn't completely believe him or understand how he could act the way he did when we were together if he didn't love me.

I agreed that I couldn't go on like this, feeling like he was slipping away and that the next time we saw each other could always be the end. Once we were together it was good, but up to that point there was too much anxiety. He didn't have an answer and clearly wasn't ending it completely, so I laid out the options as I saw them:

#1: Stop worrying about the future and just act like this is an ongoing thing. Continue to plan concerts or plays or trips in the future, so we are not just sitting around without plans every weekend, and then, if at some point in time we break up, there will be things on the calendar one of us will need to do with someone else.

#2: Take a break for a month – no communication. I am sure he will miss me and want me back. But there is also a chance that I might say 'game over' at the end of that, too. Then we get together at the end of the month and decide how to proceed.

#3: End things now.

Ball was in his court.

Of course, he couldn't decide. Maybe his feelings were as mixed up as the messages he was giving?

I said my choice would be #1, but if he couldn't make that change in mindset it had to be #2 or #3. He couldn't do #1. So, #2 or #3? And I told him not to pick #2 just because it was easier – if he thought it was going to end, I would rather just know then. I also asked if there was a chance he just hadn't been able to open up to me completely and he agreed there was that chance. So I asked him to really think about that over the next month. That happened with me earlier on with him, and when I finally opened myself up it was worth it, even though I knew I could get hurt – I asked him to try to do the same. This was at least feeling like a healthy adult conversation. Maybe I had learned some things after all?

The next step was to set ground rules for the month off:

• No communication at all until we met on the agreed-upon date.

• Communication was only allowed before then if either one of us decided it was definitely over, or if he decided it was definitely on.

I asked Tour Guide to decide what time and place we would reconvene on the specified date. He suggested Sunday morning, but I said he dumped me last time on a Sunday morning so that option was out. Ever the optimist, I suggested we go with Saturday evening and if it was a happy reunion, we could have fun. We laughed a bit about how practical I was about the whole situation and hugged and then my phone rang, and he said that was his cue to leave. Saved by the bell. (Was my life really this cliché?)

So how did I feel? Sad, but not enough to cry; tears never came. I was curious about what would happen over the next month. I was going on vacation in a week. Would I meet someone there? Would I date at all in the month? How would I feel? What would I do? That was on the one hand.

On the other hand, as soon as he left, I couldn't figure out how I would make it through the month without telling him my daily stories or listening to his. I knew I would miss those. I worried Tour Guide would crawl deep inside his head and make the wrong decision because he was overanalyzing. I worried that maybe things were not as good as I thought or as good as they should be, and I was just hanging on because it was easier than getting out there and dating again. We got along so well and had so much fun together. But did I really love him? And was that enough if Tour Guide didn't really love me? Or did I need more than that? Did I *deserve* more than that? He couldn't see a future with us together, but neither could I, if I was honest.

But I couldn't see my future in general, so did I need to be able to see our future together or could we just keep going and see? Were we putting pressure on ourselves to move forward to something that wasn't necessary? Were we trying to conform to what society thought we should do and how society thought a relationship should progress? At that point in my life, I felt we should re-write the rules of what was seen as 'normal' to what worked for our personal situation and made us happy. For me, that was a monogamous relationship with fun, respect, companionship and good sex. Basically, mental, physical and emotional chemistry and compatibility. Why wasn't that working for Tour Guide? I guess the hard part was getting two people to want to define a relationship the same way.

After all the contemplation, my next thought was to call Boy Friend and hear his thoughts, but I didn't want to tell anyone else until after the month was over. I needed to see how this played out. And I knew I needed to do that mostly on my own.

∅

THE DAY OF 'THE TALK', I WENT FOR A HIKE TO CLEAR MY HEAD AND stay calm. I was a bit anxious about the impending evening. I was trying to stay positive, thinking that would help drive a positive outcome, but I wasn't sure it would be. It was beautiful weather and I had great hike and a great day. That evening I had a 50th birthday party for one of the Gay Boyfriends planned for after 'the talk', so it was a great excuse to get all dressed up, and with my tan from vacation I was looking pretty good. Tour Guide said the same when I got to his place ... but only five minutes after I arrived, when he finally hung up the phone call he was on. He apologized profusely, saying it was an overseas call, but really, that was rude! On the flip side, Tour Guide offered me some coconut water to drink and some of my favorite snacks to eat – all things he had gone out and specially bought for me for that evening. Very thoughtful ... more mixed messages?!

The time had come. Drum roll, please ... And the answer was: Tour Guide had thought about it and decided this needed to end here.

My first thought was that I still hadn't gotten to take a picture of the full moon from up in the sky, and now it looked like I never would ... at least, not with Tour Guide. Except then he kept talking, as if nothing had just happened.

I finally let him know I needed to leave as I had a party to get to. Tour Guide seemed surprised for some reason. Was he planning to dump me and then hang out? What was I supposed to do now? Without thinking, I asked if he wanted to come with me to the party. He said yes. (Can you see the shocked expression on my face?) Shit! What had I just done?

Tour Guide asked if I REALLY wanted him to go with me. I said no, I actually didn't, but I just wasn't ready to say goodbye. He told me he wasn't either and that I could come back after the party – we could continue to talk, and he had downloaded a movie for us to watch. Sooo much confusion. Was I missing something? Who buys someone their favorite snacks and rents a movie to watch together post-break-up?

He said he would leave the door open for me and to just let myself in. And (here is the kicker), if I didn't come back, he would have his answer. I am sorry ... HE would have HIS answer? Again, did I miss something? He just broke up with me and if I didn't come back, **HE** would have **HIS** answer??? What answer would he have? What question was asked???

I had so much fun at the party with all the Gay Boyfriends, I almost forgot I had just been dumped. Like usual, they all told me how fabulous I looked and I felt surrounded by love and warmth. My spirits were lifted. And then one single straight guy walked in. Well, at that moment I didn't know he was single, but I knew he was straight because it was Ladies' Choice. What were the odds? Seriously, anyone who placed this bet would have made a lot of money. I'd never seen Ladies' Choice with this crowd of friends before – how did he get here? And how awkward would this be? And how happy was I that Tour Guide didn't end up joining me!

I wasn't sure if Ladies' Choice remembered me (why on earth did I think he wouldn't remember?). When I made it his way to say hello, he clearly remembered me but didn't actually use my name, so I wasn't sure if he remembered that. I learned after we spoke that he used to work with one of the women there and she invited him along because he was going through a nasty break-up (presumably with the woman he was seeing when we were seeing each other ... funny that, huh?). One of my best Gay Boyfriends said to her, "That's funny, Julie is going through a break-up right now as we speak." Ha-ha. Life is funny, life is cruel, life is darn right entertaining ... well, at least in my world. So how does one reply to a comment like that? "Let him know I'm available for casual sex if he's interested." There might not have been a lot there with Ladies' Choice, but the sex was good and I was pretty sure I was about to hit a dry spell, so what the heck.

Yes, after leaving the party, rather than going home I drove back to see Tour Guide, who was watching a movie. He motioned for me to join him and we sat snuggled up until it was finished and went to bed. Of course! Isn't this what happens after a break-up after a 30-day break? In the morning there was no discussion of what had happened or what would happen going forward. Not even another mixed message; no message.

I got into my car and checked my phone. I had a text from just after I left the party saying, "It was really good to see you." Apparently Ladies' Choice remembered my name *and* my number.

✍

FLIRTING, EMAILS, TEXTS, NOTHING, DATES, MORE NOTHING – ALL
with Tour Guide. And then, a conversation that I should date other
people. Tour Guide told me he wasn't dating anyone and he wouldn't
because he needed time to mourn the end of one thing before moving
on. (But had this actually ended?) I, on the other hand, since there was
no commitment, felt dating helped keep my mind from wandering to
destructive and crazy-making thoughts about what Tour Guide was
doing when we weren't together.

I went out with Ladies' Choice a few times but just wasn't into it.
Conveniently, Kentucky and 31 came back around too, but I passed
on getting together with them because I knew if I had to have the "I
slept with someone else" conversation, *everything* would end, and I
still didn't want that to happen … yet. So I kept my pants on.

I believe Tour Guide did too, although there were a few telltale signs
that he may have been dating. A red hair in *my* headset for the plane, a
pair of earrings in the guest bathroom. Explanations from Tour Guide
that, while plausible, I just didn't believe. It breaks my heart to think he
would lie to me. But the question is, was he actually lying to me or did
he think he was sparing me from the sorts of details he also didn't want
to know about from me? If he really knew me, he would know I prefer
to know the truth than to be lied to or deceived. But he seemed to be
better at looking at things like that from his own point of view rather
than mine. And, of course, all of the questioning brought on bouts of
anxiety as I allowed my mind to wander and distrust.

Becoming the dumper

I couldn't live in this limbo land any longer; it was time to move on. It was time for the final talk. I told Tour Guide I was still seeing him because I wanted us to be more than just friends. I reminded him that when there was sex and a physical relationship, in my mind it was more than just a friendship, and I worried that even with that he was now looking at us as "just friends". He didn't deny it. As much as I didn't want it, it seemed "yet" had now arrived.

"You are a pretty amazing guy, but I'm also a pretty amazing girl and I finally realize I *do* deserve more than what this is right now. I don't think you can find anyone better suited for you, so if you wake up one day and realize that, please don't let pride get in the way of calling me." He had a hard time looking at me while I was saying all of this and he didn't stop me when I got up and walked out. So there it was, the end.

Driving home, all I could think was, *I know I did the right thing, but it sure doesn't feel like it.* The tears didn't come, though, they rarely do. All those years of being told to stop crying left me bottling it up on the inside rather than letting it out.

I still have a really hard time believing Tour Guide wasn't in love with me. The way he acted towards me all the way through and the things he said and did always left me utterly astonished and confused by his protests of deep emotion. Maybe he was fooling himself, or maybe I was fooling myself; I don't think we'll ever know which it was. Perhaps a little of both? But I put myself out there, raw, open, vulnerable, in a way I hadn't done before, and for that opportunity I am grateful. I only wish Tour Guide was able to do the same, because in my heart of hearts I think he just wasn't able to open himself up to being vulnerable in a way that also opened him up to the possibility of being hurt.

$$\mathcal{L}$$

IT WAS TIME TO CONCENTRATE ON BEING HAPPY ON MY OWN. A WISE woman told me that part of what I liked so much about Tour Guide was how wonderful I looked through his eyes. It was time for me to step back and get comfortable seeing myself like that through my own eyes. It was time to do that, and to figure out some answers to questions I had for myself ...

Did I really want to be with Tour Guide because of who he was, or was I hanging on just because I couldn't have him? Was he really the right guy for me or were the good and exciting parts just outshining the negatives? Was he just part of my healing process from my divorce, helping me to see I could have someone in my life who treated me well, and he was just a stepping stone to opening me up to that? Was there someone else out there who could provide everything he did and more? Did he actually provide as much as I thought he did, or was I just overly generous in my thinking of how he treated me?

Lots to think about.

CHAPTER THIRTEEN

Exploration

BY THE TIME THINGS WERE COMPLETELY OVER WITH TOUR GUIDE, things online were very different. It's amazing how quickly things changed in the online dating world. When I started dating Tour Guide, there was no such thing as mobile dating apps, and by the time that ended, there was a new app called Blendr that was said to be the straight version of Grindr. There was also OkCupid, which didn't have a mobile app yet, and before you know it, Tinder was all the rage. And after that, Bumble then Hinge and so many others too.

There seemed to be certain trends that followed the addition of each new app. Each seemed to start with a younger crowd, and as it gained in popularity, it would age up. There would be just a few guys in my age range and each month that would increase. I'd see the same guys on multiple apps so even though one app might be known more for hook-ups and another more for relationships, it seemed to depend more on the guy than the platform. Whenever I'd start an account with a new app, the first handful of profiles shown to me were super attractive … and then they would get less so. If I'd go away from the app for a while and then come back, it would have the same pattern, always starting with the most attractive men and going downhill from there.

Did they do this to reward me for coming back, or to draw me back in? I am not naïve enough to think it was coincidence; somehow, they worked their algorithms to make that happen. Rumors of attractiveness scores built into the algorithms have floated around, but the apps always deny that is the case. Maybe they just base it on the percentage of swipes right versus left? Any way you look at it, it feels heavily based on looks and quantity of profiles rather than quality and substance.

Patterns

There were other interesting patterns that seemed to be particular to me rather than to the dating app population at large. I don't know if this was coincidence or if it had something to do with what I was attracting into my space for some kind of life lesson I needed to decipher. A category of men would all show up at one time – smokers, dads, unemployed, cheaters, tall guys, short guys, bald guys, older guys, younger guys, realtors … You name it, I would get a handful of matches in one week that all seemed to fall into a pattern. Was this happening to other people too, or just me? It was as if the universe was throwing patterns my way to help me determine what I did and definitely didn't want in a relationship.

The first pattern I noticed was smokers. I am not only not a fan of smoking, but just a hint of the smell of cigarettes makes me feel so queasy I wouldn't even consider meeting a smoker for a quick meet and greet. I knew there was no way I would ever kiss a man who tasted like an ashtray. Yuck!

So how did I end up on multiple meet and greets with smokers? They hadn't copped to being a smoker until we were already on the meet and greet. Had they been learning that non-smoking women like me wouldn't match with them, so they kept it out of their profile thinking we might like their personality enough to ignore it? As much as I wanted to be open to anything, this experience reassured me that smoking is an actual deal-breaker for me. If you'd like to date me, quit smoking first!

The patterns got a bit more interesting – or risqué, depending on how you look at it. One week I found people looking for a third. Funnily enough, I was approached to be a third offline in addition to experiencing this pattern online. The first offline experience happened at a party and I was a bit naïve and didn't fully recognize it for what it was at the time. The second time some of the Gay Boyfriends invited me over to meet a friend of theirs. They didn't tell me she was interviewing me to be a third for her and her boyfriend. I'm glad they didn't share that tidbit until after she left. I told them I was flattered they'd think of me, but no thanks. What was the universe telling me? Was that something I needed to explore? Or just helping me determine where my boundaries were? I opted for the latter.

The next pattern I entered into unwittingly. It started with open marriages and progressed to polyamory ...

Sexual dynamics

I'd been getting used to seeing the patterns, so I shouldn't have been surprised when match after match told me they were in open relationships. I asked one, "So, does your wife know you're in an open relationship?"

"Good question, actually, no she doesn't."

I had to break the news to him: he wasn't actually in an open relationship; he was just cheating on his wife. Are people really stupid enough to think that ploy works, or stupid enough to fall for it? Of course, he then thought I should reward him for his newfound honesty by meeting him. Seriously?

Another guy who genuinely seemed to be in an open relationship kept asking me to meet him. I wasn't really interested, but I was curious how it all worked, so I finally agreed to meet him. I was up-front with him that it was curiosity, not interest that led me to finally agree to meet him and there would be nothing past a meet and greet. Surprisingly, he agreed to the terms.

I didn't hold back. Right away I started with the questions, and he was forthcoming with answers. After a few years of marriage, he got bored and spoke to his wife about opening the relationship. She said no, and he said he wanted a divorce then. She loved him and didn't want to lose him, so she agreed to the open relationship.

"No," he said in response to my asking if she was seeing other people too. She didn't want to. Somehow, without him describing her, I could see her. She was pretty, but not gorgeous, and I saw her sitting at home, crying and anxious, despairing over the fact she was not enough for this man she loved. When he'd come home from another rendezvous and they'd eat dinner, she'd push the food around her plate and could barely chew or swallow.

She was holding back the tears and trying to be positive and whimsical and entertaining so he would still love her and stay. But there was a sinking pit in the bottom of her stomach filled with the worry and the knowing that one day he would come home and tell her he'd found someone else he wanted more. My heart broke for her as I wondered why she couldn't see what I saw so clearly – she deserved more for herself than this man who allowed her to stay in an unhappy marriage that served him well but was slowly breaking her.

I'd like to think I wouldn't allow that to happen to me in a relationship, but I can see parts of myself in her, which is why I think I saw her so clearly. I lose myself in wanting *him* to want me so much that I don't even know who I am or what I want, or notice when he isn't treating me the way I deserve to be treated. Is that the answer to all my questions about my relationship with Tour Guide?

In that moment, with that man – this woman's husband – I felt strong; I had a voice. I could see him clearly for what he was and had no desire for him or fear of being hurt by him. So, for her, and for myself too, when he continued to try to convince me I was lucky to have met him and it would be a good thing for me to sleep with him because he was so good in bed, I said: "So let me make sure I understand you. You are saying that you are the one who has something to offer me? That as a single woman, I should be happy that you, a married man, in an open relationship that is breaking your wife's heart, are offering me the gift of having sex with you, on a regular basis if I would like, and that this is a good deal for me?" The smile on his face told me he thought I was about to agree – he wasn't going to want to hear what I had to say next. "First of all, it is clear you are causing your wife a lot of pain and sadness, and I won't be party to hurting another woman in a way I hope will never happen to me. Second of all, I am single and interested in meeting someone where there is a possibility of something, so why would I settle for a married man? And third of all, if I just want good sex, which I don't even know you'd be able to provide, wouldn't it make sense for me to say yes to one of the hot young single guys that are constantly messaging me?"

Can you believe after all that he still texted me for weeks after we met trying to get me to reconsider and have sex with him?

ॐ

AND THEN, AS A MATTER OF COURSE, I MOVED ON FROM A PATTERN of open marriage to polyamory. Seems like a fairly natural progression, right? I didn't actually know much about it. Fortunately, I went to Burning Man, where I learned about polyamory offline before the pattern continued online.

Before we get into the polyamory, I need to make a plug for taking yourself to somewhere like Burning Man. It was the most amazing experience. Being away from the 'default world', as the burners call it, I was able to let go a bit and be free from worrying so much about what others thought. Everyone out there was doing their own thing, and no one seemed to notice or care what I looked like or what I was doing. I learned that I was physically and emotionally stronger than I realized, as I stepped into the principles of radical self-reliance, self-expression and inclusion. I was outside of my comfort zone almost the entire time I was there, and I found a piece of myself there that had been missing: an ability to just be and feel and express vulnerability and live without the need to control everything. And while many others partake, for me, all of this was done without any drugs or sex and a minimal amount of alcohol. Not that I'm against any of that, just that I had thrown myself into such a foreign way of being that I don't think I could have handled substances on top of that. I highly recommend everyone experience a place like this at least once in a lifetime. If your experience is anything like mine, you will thank me.

One evening, I sat down to have a chat with a campmate in the next tent. He'd been going to Burning Man for years and was happy to spend some time with a newbie. I asked if he was married or had kids and he said yes to both. He also said he was polyamorous. At the time, that was a new word for me and I was curious. He told me that in addition to his wife (whom he termed his primary relationship) and a son, he had a longtime girlfriend, and his wife had another partner as well. I had a lot of questions and he had a lot of answers.

"Isn't there jealousy?"

"No, there is compersion."

"What is that?"

"It's when you derive pleasure from your loved one getting pleasure from sex or a relationship with someone else."

I've never been a particularly jealous person, but my brain just doesn't comprehend the definition of that word. I can't imagine myself experiencing compersion, even though I went on to experiment with polyamory ... to a certain extent. I didn't actually intend to experiment in this realm, it just happened that the polyamorous pattern happened by meeting two men who hadn't divulged this status in their profile, and then one who kind of did. Wouldn't it make more sense to share information like that in a profile? Perhaps they liked the idea of recruiting new members into the world of polyamory. Or are polyamorous relationships not always as open and honest as some would portray them to be?

The Adonis

I woke up to see the naked backside of one of the most beautiful men I'd ever seen. He'd just climbed out of my bed and was stretching his arms above his head on his way to the bathroom. I could see a partial reflection of the front of The Adonis in the full-length mirror across the room. I loved having this man in my life and in my bed – and out of it, too, because we had such deep, meaningful conversations and were so entirely connected. I felt like the only person in his world because The Adonis focused 100 percent on me and made me feel I was all that existed even though everyone in the room, male and female, was looking at him as they walked by. The Adonis didn't even seem to notice.

From the moment we met and his arm brushed against mine across the table at the coffee shop, I felt electricity. The Adonis didn't mention it in his profile, but sitting at the table talking, he was quite open that he was poly. He was seeing a few different *people* (I didn't realize at the time the non-gendered term was used on purpose) but he didn't have a primary at the moment. I wasn't sure if this situation was going to be for me, but I was drawn to The Adonis and knew I wanted to see him again. We fell into a pattern of seeing each other about once a week. I never asked what he was doing when he wasn't with me, and The Adonis never offered. I tried my best not to ask questions I didn't think I wanted answers to. And yes, that does sometimes bite me on the butt.

Before one of our dates, The Adonis told me he needed to run an errand and asked if I wanted to meet later or come along. I agreed to go along and found myself in a sex shop with The Adonis pulling out a silicone dildo that was larger than anything I had ever seen and almost certainly at least three times the size of any living form. He nonchalantly removed it from the box and showed the shop owner how there was a tear between the balls and the shaft that shouldn't have happened so soon after purchase. I was doing my best to hold my composure and seem just as cool and relaxed as he was. I tried not to visualize the answers to the questions I had in my head. *What in the world were you doing with that, where did you put it, and how did it break?*

Our little romance continued for a few months until I moved away. Over that time, it appeared I was getting better at separating sex from a relationship and having a pretty successful fling. I never let The Adonis know that when we became Facebook friends I could see that at the time we'd met he did indeed have a primary, and I saw pictures of the engagement ring he gave her just before we started dating. I felt a tinge of jealousy but not more than that – likely because I knew what we had was casual and by the time I discovered the fiancée I knew I'd be moving away. I definitely did not feel compersion, though. What I didn't understand was why, if The Adonis was openly poly and so readily open about so many things, did he decide to lie to me about that? I was proud of myself for pondering these things in a somewhat detached manner rather than calling him out on the lie. Could I take this new learning and skill with me into an actual relationship? Or was this actually just another case of not standing up for myself? I have no idea what his fiancée knew or didn't know about his omission.

The Coach

While I was definitely smitten with The Adonis, with The Coach I always felt a bit uneasy and a little uncomfortable too. I could never quite decide if that was because he challenged me to be real with myself and to learn and grow, or if it was that he carefully disguised arrogance and condescension under the guise of caring and guiding. I continued to see him as an exercise in personal growth and instinctually knew I needed to learn something from this interaction. It was also an interesting dichotomy to be dating both of these men at the same time and experience how different it felt to spend time with each of them.

I don't think The Coach was seeing anyone else at the time, or at least not seeing anyone seriously, but he did make it clear that he was poly. He didn't ask, so I didn't tell him I was seeing The Adonis; I did tell him polyamory wasn't something that interested me, and I had recently learned about compersion but didn't think that was an emotion in my vocabulary. He couldn't understand my point of view any more than I could relate to his, so I explained. "When you come home on a Friday evening and I say I'm so glad you're home because I've had a tough week and just want to have a great night out with you – oh and I'm feeling horny too, and you tell me, 'Sorry but I have a date tonight', I'm not going to be happy for you. I'm going to be pissed off and disappointed and hurt."

"No you won't, because I would want you to be happy so I'd say, 'That's okay, let me call one of my friends who will take you out and show you a good time.'"

Yuck. Let me see if I've got this right: the guy I'm seeing doesn't want me to be upset and unsatisfied, so since he has a date with another woman, he is going to pimp me out to his friend? This definitely isn't for me. I chose not to test his level of compersion out by telling him about The Adonis.

☏

FROM MY BRUSHES WITH POLYAMORY, I LEARNED SOMETHING ABOUT my boundaries when it came to sex and relationships and what I *don't* want. I appreciated both of these men for coming into my life and helping me to gain clarity on that. The most beautiful thing about both of them was that we remained friends and are in contact every now and again. I saw each of them when I last went back to visit. The Adonis was in a monogamous relationship (not with the previous fiancée) and was quite content. He explained to me that he has plenty of love to go around for multiple people, but there just wasn't enough time to divide up across all of them – after all, you only have one birthday every year, so who do you spend that with? The Coach was married – I met his wife, who was lovely, and they seemed very happy together. We weren't in the right setting to ask if they were monogamous and, really, that isn't my business, but I get the feeling they are.

Not So Poly

"I'm ethically polyamorous," read a profile I came across after my move. With my new knowledge of polyamory and more fully understanding of my boundaries, I was curious. I couldn't help myself, I had to reply. "Can you help me understand what that means?"

Not So Poly explained to me, "Well, I am in a relationship with someone and we have agreed to see other people as well, so she has another guy that she sees too."

"And you? How many other women are you seeing?"

"Well, I haven't really seen anyone other than her."

I then shared with Not So Poly that really, then, he was in a monogamous relationship with a woman who was poly, and there wasn't actually a thing as ethically poly because by the very nature of its definition, polyamory was ethical – and the opposite of ethical in this situation would be that you were cheating on your partner.

Not So Poly enjoyed the conversations we were having so we continued chatting. I shared with him some resources he might like to look into, including a talk with Esther Perel and Dan Savage on the topic. It turned out I was enjoying the conversation too. Not So Poly was smart and insightful and willing to listen and explore. I agreed to meet him for a drink, being very clear that polyamory wasn't an option for me. We spent a bit more time together and while I enjoyed getting to know Not So Poly, I let him know I wasn't willing for things to go further because polyamory wasn't for me. What *I heard* Not So Poly say after that was that he was thinking of ending it with the other woman anyhow, and he led me to believe that was happening. What I *thought* was that this could possibly come to something then.

Based on my understanding, yep, we got naked. Nope, things didn't end with the other woman. Had I heard him wrong or did Not So Poly lead me astray?

I had learned and I had grown and I was ready to stand up for myself and what I wanted. I wasn't going to let it linger or see what *could* happen. I asked Not So Poly to meet me for breakfast and told him I was sad and hurt that he misled me and that I was done. I had been clear from the beginning I had no interest in entering into a polyamorous situation, so this was now over. Somehow, he wasn't expecting that conversation at all. Was I misled or had I misunderstood? I didn't ask for greater clarification and he didn't push me to change my mind. We didn't stop speaking altogether, though, and Not So Poly and I became friends over time. He and the other woman he was seeing are now seeing each other exclusively.

What is it with me and polyamory? I seem to turn polyamorous men into friends for me and great monogamous partners for someone else. Growing up, I used to dream of the hot bad boy suddenly turning into an adoring boyfriend. Is that why this kept happening? Did I need to be clearer that I wanted him to turn into *my* boyfriend, not some other woman's? Still, it felt like I was making progress in determining what I wanted in a relationship and showing up for myself. So, I guess there was that.

CHAPTER FOURTEEN

Looking for an equal partnership

I'D HAD ENOUGH OF THE PATTERNS AND THE MEET AND GREETS; I was ready for something more substantial. And, while I found myself *feeling* ready for that, perhaps I still had some more work to do on identifying a suitable partner. Or maybe I had some more work left to do on understanding my own value enough to be ready and willing to *wait* for a truly suitable partner. It wasn't even until the end of the relationship with Tour Guide that I could even begin to see more clearly how things were always on his terms, and when they weren't, he would behave badly. Yes, he planned amazing experiences that seemed so thoughtful, but then I'd ask him to come along to something I wanted to do and he would pout. What was it going to take for me to actually step up to that equal partnership I wanted and find someone else to step up with me?

Being someone's everything

Young Boyfriend seemed cute, funny and ambitious. In addition to his day job, he was working on starting his own business and seemed to like to get out and explore new places, to go walking and take photos. He was also a decade younger than me, so I was shying away from going out with him. He kept messaging me and kept me laughing, so after a while I finally agreed to meet him. I figured with the age difference nothing big would happen, but if there was chemistry on the meet and greet, perhaps a fling?

The chemistry was there. But I made a tactical mistake: I allowed it to transform from a fling to a relationship.

How did I allow this to happen? At the time, I would have answered that it was fun and easy and Young Boyfriend was eager to please in bed, so why not just continue and enjoy? I was far enough along in life where I wasn't going to be having children, and he didn't want kids, so what was stopping us from continuing and enjoying each other's company?

I perhaps enjoyed Young Boyfriend's adoration a little too much, and before you know it, we had a full-blown relationship. Young Boyfriend was quite happy to fit into my life because, let's face it, my life – including where I lived, my friends, my lifestyle – were a lot more evolved than his. Before I could see it happening, his life completely revolved around me. We did what I wanted, with whom I wanted, when I wanted. Sounds heavenly? It is … until it is not. Having someone's life revolve around you sounds good in theory. At first it feels really nice to have someone who will be there for anything you want to do and available to you whenever you desire. But when you realize they are *always* there, and *always* just waiting, it feels like a heavy weight to carry and a lot of responsibility. When someone doesn't have enough of their own life and own desires, that doesn't feel good.

As the months passed by, Young Boyfriend's ambition faded. His minimum-wage job meant that if I wanted to go to dinner at a nice restaurant or away for a weekend, I paid. He didn't automatically expect me to cover costs, but he couldn't afford to do the things I wanted to do, and I didn't want to stop doing them. When I wanted to fly out for a friend's birthday weekend, Young Boyfriend told me he couldn't afford to come along and he didn't want me to have to pay for him.

We had a seemingly mature and adult conversation about it. I explained that I didn't want to go alone, I wanted my boyfriend with me, and if that meant covering the cost for him, that still made me happier than going without him. We ended up going and it was truly a better weekend because he was there with me.

Young Boyfriend said he'd had a talk with his mom and asked her what a successful, together woman like me wanted with a guy like him – and she told him companionship, which was not always easy to find. She made sense; she was mostly right. He asked if it bothered me that he didn't have money or a career and I said not at that point, but I would let him know if that changed.

ℒ

A FEW MONTHS LATER, I WOKE UP AND FELT THE PRESSURE. THE positive side of this relationship was no longer outweighing the weight of it. I realized I had somehow become responsible for two people's lives. I was doing all the cooking, shopping, planning and decision-making for both of us. Young Boyfriend chipped in with what he could offer – he did dishes, installed closet organizers and was a warm body in my bed. I had the freedom to go out and see my friends on my own or with him, but it was always my friends, my place, my brainpower, my money for everything. I wanted a partner who could match me not just with the finances but also the brainpower to handle everyday decisions, make plans and offer sound insights when I needed to talk through things that were going on at work. It became all too clear I didn't have a partner to support me in this way or who had the same desire to continue to learn and grow. Without this, my life and career were starting to stagnate.

It wasn't enough. I wanted more from life. I didn't want to break Young Boyfriend's heart, but my perspective on us had changed. I'd told him I would let him know if and when that happened. The time had come.

Young Boyfriend didn't take the news well. I understood; he was hurt. So was I. But I was hurting myself and my life, and likely his too, by continuing this. I wanted, needed and deserved an equal partner and, unfortunately for both of us, that wasn't Young Boyfriend.

ॐ

COULD I HAVE HANDLED THIS BETTER? ABSOLUTELY. I COULD HAVE left it at a fling and not gotten involved or allowed him to either. In hindsight, I blame my natural proclivity towards thinking having sex with someone means we should be in a relationship. Not to mention my inability to consider sex as a bit of fun that should be allowed to run its course before we smile, part ways and carry on with life. "Good sex does not equal good relationship" is a lesson that seems to continue to escape me.

At least I had the sense to end things before they deteriorated to the point where we hurt each other more than was necessary. I'd like to think I enriched his life by being in it. Experiencing this type of relationship dynamic definitely enriched mine. I felt loved unconditionally by Young Boyfriend and did my best to love him back the same way, but I don't think I was as successful. That's something I want to work on when I have the opportunity again. Equal partnership has always been something I've desired in a relationship, but now I have a better understanding of why it is important and what I want it to look like and feel like. Most importantly, I learned that allowing someone else to revolve their life completely around yours isn't good for either party, and while it might sound fun to dream about or talk about, it isn't something I ever want in a relationship – in either direction.

Living someone else's life

I feel like my life is a pendulum sometimes and I go from one extreme to the other. I swung from a younger guy with not much going on in his life to one who was a bit older than me, who had three kids from two ex-wives and 50/50 custody of the two younger ones who were still school-aged and living at home. Reflecting on my last two relationships and the dates I had been on since then, I wanted to focus on being open and generous and allowing myself to jump in and feel without worrying about getting hurt. I wanted an equal partnership, and I was hoping The Dad would be the opportunity for all of that.

♌

THE DAD AND I QUICKLY PROGRESSED FROM A MEET AND GREET TO A first date and forward from there. I was open and honest about what I was looking for and that was reciprocated. It seemed we were on the right path. I was enjoying the time we were spending together, and while my openness and vulnerability in sharing with him didn't come easily or naturally, it felt like real personal growth and like I was doing this well. Check, check, check. Time to move things forward.

I invited The Dad over for dinner and he asked if it would be okay to bring an overnight bag so he didn't have to drive late at night after drinking. He was perfectly happy to stay in my guest room if that would be most comfortable for me. That was sweet and gentlemanly, but in my mind, it was time to add sex into the equation. Dinner at home without the interruptions of waiters, other patrons to look at and noise all around was the perfect way to get to know each other better and allow things to progress.

We shared our personal histories and what The Dad shared with me rang warning bells loud and clear. I didn't see that coming. It wasn't the direction I'd thought it would take. It appeared I had again attracted a man with a lot of emotional baggage he hadn't yet unpacked. This didn't sound like he was the type of man I wanted to be getting into a relationship with. But he'd packed his overnight bag. Hmmm ...

We'd drunk enough wine with dinner that it was clear The Dad wouldn't be driving home, so that wasn't an option. Yes, he had mentioned my guest room and the smart thing for me to do would have been to put him in there. But that felt awkward and I didn't want the awkwardness, so I offered for him to just stay in my bed. I made it clear we would only be sleeping, and he agreed. We had a bit of a smooch goodnight and went to sleep. Perfect; all was well. In the morning I could send The Dad on his way and let him down gently when he was back in the safety of his own suburb.

Wrong. There are some mistakes I haven't gotten smart enough not to repeat. Morning came and having a warm body in bed with me all night got the juices flowing. While I had made it clear there would be no sex that night, apparently I hadn't factored in that my body would take over and erase what my mind so clearly knew when I felt a warm, clearly aroused man wrapped around me in the morning.

Unfortunately, the sex was really good and I experienced an intimate connection like nothing I could remember experiencing previously. And yes, being who I am, I confused sexual intimacy and connection with emotional intimacy and connection. Hindsight allowed me to see that confusion clearly, but you can bet I didn't at the time. <sigh>

Pow! I was right in it, ready to explore a relationship with a man I was more than ready to say goodbye to less than 24 hours earlier. In fact, I was 100 percent clear at bedtime that The Dad was not at all relationship material. Where did my brain and common sense go? I've heard that men think with their dicks – I've never heard anyone say that women think with their vaginas but maybe there is some truth in that too. It's probably more accurate to say that sex caused temporary amnesia, wiping out the pertinent information from the night before and my usual common sense.

♌

I WAS READY TO GIVE THIS BUDDING RELATIONSHIP MY ALL. I WAS all in, practicing loving unconditionally and being non-judgmental and accepting a person as they are. I was doing my best to give of myself readily and openly, without fear of getting hurt. In my head, this was all going really well. I met The Dad's best friend and I was given the thumbs up. And then I was out walking one day and he called and said, "I was just thinking, before this goes much further, I need to know how you would feel about being a stepmom and living in the suburbs. I don't need you to answer that now, I just need you to take some time and think about it. That's why I'm having this conversation with you on the phone rather than in person, so you have some time and space."

He caught me at the perfect time because being out walking in nature helps me process. The first thing I thought was, *He handled that conversation well and is being very considerate of my needs. Awww, I like him even more.* My next thought: *He likes me, he really, really likes me, he wants me to seriously think about being in his and his girls' lives forever. Maybe I have lived a city lifestyle full of city friends and eating at great restaurants and traveling the world for all these years already and that was enough. Maybe I've had enough of that lifestyle or even too much of that lifestyle and would be happier and more fulfilled moving to the suburbs and being a stepmom and having a family.* And I started, in my mind, redecorating his home and remodeling so that I could be happy living in his house. We hadn't even said "I love you" yet at that point. How did I let myself get so carried away? Was it simply because in that conversation, without The Dad actually saying the words, I heard that he wanted me?

Our next date was amazing. It had been a while since we'd seen each other and the chemistry was definitely there. Before we knew it, clothes were on the ground. After that, I told him about an article I'd read about the "36 Questions That Lead to Love" and we went through the questions over a glass of wine in my living room. Physical and emotional intimacy *and* connection – checkmate. We finished up and headed out to dinner, and then dancing to a great band that was playing not too far from my place. He was a great dancer and he whispered in my ear that he loved the way I moved on the dance floor. Could this night get any better?

I ran off to the ladies' room and returned to find him sitting on a stool at the bar. I snuck up behind him thinking I would kiss his neck romantically and stopped abruptly as I saw he was on Tinder. WTF? The last few hours we'd been connecting in every way and on every level, and I walked away for two minutes and came back to find him on Tinder *while* we were still on a date? WTF?! Which is exactly what I said to him. "We've had this amazing night, and I thought we were seeing each other exclusively. Earlier this week you asked me to make sure I could see myself fitting into your life and I've done all of that and you are on Tinder in the middle of our date?"

It was a mistake, he told me. His phone pinged and he checked to see if his girls texted and saw there was a notification from Tinder. He hadn't been on it forever, he didn't even realize it was on his phone, this was just an old connection that had messaged him; he'd gladly erase the app. I chose to stay in the happy bubble of our beautiful evening, so I believed him. I was all in – I wanted this to be the truth.

⅋

I MET THE DAD'S DAUGHTERS AND THEY APPROVED WHOLEHEARTEDLY. I had been taking some time off work to explore the possibility of starting my own business, so my schedule was flexible and I was able to help him out with the girls when he got into a bind. It started feeling like we could be a family. In my mind, everything with this relationship was going well.

Out of nowhere, I was offered a job with some people I'd worked with before. Unlike my last relationship, I now had a partner I could talk to and work through the pros and cons of taking the job – an equal partner to provide the support I needed. I didn't at the time see how much that idea blinded me to the reality. I didn't see that The Dad liked the idea of a paycheck and job security more than I did, or that I allowed that to influence my decision to take the job rather than follow my passion. I was literally so blinded by the idea of this man and this relationship and the family we could have together that, without realizing it, I was losing myself in a relationship that at the beginning I didn't think I should enter into.

It took a good friend to open my eyes. I was staying at The Dad's house, watching his dog and cats while he was away for a few days. My friend came over for breakfast. I was cooking away as his cat walked across the counter. Normally I would be totally disgusted by a cat on the counter where I was cooking, and my friend knew that. Unphased by her smirking face, I continued, but she wasn't going to let it go. She could see clearly what I couldn't.

"Julie, what are you doing? You can't live here, you can't live like this. You have a beautiful home and a beautiful life. You move here and half your income goes into fixing up a home he hasn't maintained for over a decade so that you'd feel comfortable living here and it could be even nearly as nice as your home. He hasn't been on vacation for years because he can't afford it and now, rather than going on vacation, you'll be paying for his kids' college – and if you do manage a vacation, you'll be paying for his kids to come along. *And* you'd be moving to a place where you have no friends and no support around you. *And* all that is well and good if this is a real partnership with give and take, but what is he giving up for you? Where is his compromise? From what you've said, you are barely seeing him because he plays in three different sports leagues on top of his responsibility with the girls and his job, and isn't willing to back off from any of that. What is he giving you in return for all that you are giving him?"

How had I never seen that? How did I get to this place where I was so willing to please that I didn't see The Dad wasn't giving anything of himself, but I was giving everything? How had I lost myself yet again? I thought I was coming into this with such strength and openness in a way I hadn't given of myself before in a relationship. And perhaps I was, but I forgot to look at the other side of the equation.

And even with all of that, *he* ended the relationship, not me. I was heartbroken. It seemed with all that I gave, I still wasn't enough for this man. I was crushed. Would I ever measure up, would I ever be enough? If I was truly honest with myself, I knew The Dad didn't measure up to anything I needed or deserved. Why didn't I pay attention to that? Did he see that? Is that why he ended things?

Am I smart enough now? Have I learned that I need to factor myself into the equal partnership and see my own value and make sure a partner measures up to what I deserve? I'd like to think so, but I am not sure I am wholly there yet. It was time to step back *again* and figure out how I could show up for myself. How many times did I need to learn this lesson? And why was I not better at this?

The Mentor

After all of that, I took a bit of a break from dating. I needed to recover, mentally and emotionally. I needed to understand better how I could think I was so ready to enter into an equal partnership when they weren't turning out to be equal at all. After some time away from dating, I came to understand the relationship I had been needing to develop was with myself. I had always been comfortable spending time with myself, but now I *really* got comfortable with being with myself, getting to know myself and what I wanted and who I wanted to be. Developing this relationship felt like it was the key to dating more successfully. I got to a point where I became less attached to the outcome of interactions and meet and greets. Poor behavior still pissed me off, but it wasn't affecting me the way it used to. Given my newfound state of being, it's not surprising that at this point in time I met The Mentor.

The Mentor's first message to me showed that he had actually read my profile. I always like when someone looks past the pictures; it says something about them as a person. He had a "…" in his profile and I asked what that meant. Turned out, The Mentor was in town on business weekly and not looking for a relationship, just a dinner companion with good conversation. I asked if he had a relationship back home and he said that he did, to which I replied that I was open to dinner and good conversation but nothing more. He agreed.

So many conversations and meet and greets went nowhere that dinner with someone I could see was intelligent and could possibly be a friend sounded good. A smart new boy friend seemed like a good idea. We had good friend chemistry from the first moment, which lead to easy conversation, making it seem that we had known each other for some time. We talked about the world, travel, work … we were not ever at a loss for conversation points. And then I asked about his relationship. The Mentor had an ex-wife and kids. They'd split a few years ago, he'd met a woman who he'd been in a relationship with since, and they were currently building a house together. Sounded nice, something I wouldn't mind for myself, actually … Maybe he had a nice single friend to introduce me to?

And then it got really interesting. What was The Mentor doing on a dating app, then? Seemed like an odd place to find just a dinner companion? It turned out he and his girlfriend were swingers and decided that while he was away on business, they could each 'play' separately – no use depriving themselves of sex because of logistics. Yes, definitely interesting … but just to learn about, not something I wanted to explore.

So many questions came to mind and The Mentor was more than willing to answer them. The relationship he had with his wife had been fairly standard, but right from the start of the relationship with the girlfriend they decided to open it up and swing. It was her idea. He took to it quickly and loved playing the strait-laced businessman by day and swinger by night. They would dress up in sexy clothing and attend swinger parties. They also had a group of swinger friends they vacationed with. This group loved to go out to restaurants, switch partners during dinner and watch the restaurant staff squirm and try to figure out what was going on. They preferred mature swingers to newbies because newbies sometimes couldn't handle the emotion of it and The Mentor didn't like the drama.

If The Mentor was at a party in a room where the sex wasn't good, he would just get up in the middle of it and walk out. That was the part of the conversation I gasped at. I couldn't imagine the horror of someone walking out on me mid-act because it just wasn't very good. "Why settle for bad sex when there is so much good sex available?" was his answer. What he enjoyed about swinging was that everyone knew what they liked and what they wanted, and gave and took direction well, so it was most often a very pleasurable experience.

"What do you like?" he asked. I blushed. I'd never been comfortable with that topic of conversation.

The Mentor seemed to enjoy my interest and my questions and let me know that if I wanted to take the conversation into the bedroom, he found me attractive and would be happy to do that. I said thank you, but no, not my cup of tea to be intimate with a man who was already in a relationship. He understood, so we called it a night and he asked if I'd like to have dinner again the following week. Clearly, we both enjoyed the conversation and the new friendship developing even if there wasn't to be any sex. Learning more about swinging helped further clarify my personal boundaries.

Or so I thought …

𝕤

ABOUT A WEEK LATER, I WAS TALKING WITH A GIRLFRIEND. SHE TOLD me she was seeing a new guy and it was casual, but the sex was mind-blowing. I could barely remember the last time I'd had mind-blowing sex … hmph, let's be honest, I could barely remember the last time I'd had sex. That got me thinking … Maybe it was time for me to learn to get comfortable asking for what I wanted? And maybe it would be comfortable for me to experiment with that with a man who I wasn't looking to enter into a relationship with?

The first thing I noticed when I met The Mentor for dinner the following week was the addition of a wedding ring. I was 100 percent sure he wasn't wearing one last time we met. I asked about that – I was fairly certain he hadn't said he was married. No, but he hadn't said he wasn't. His explanation was that he wasn't trying to hide anything, but he found the ring could be off-putting when he first met someone. On the one hand, I was thinking, *Fair enough.* On the other hand, I was thinking, *Yeah, but not completely honest.* And when I finished weighing out the balance of each hand in my mind, I decided this wasn't about him so much as it was about me and what I wanted, so I would go ahead with my plan.

Halfway through dinner I said to The Mentor, "I was thinking about our talk last week. I've never had a mentor in my life, but as you know I've been a mentor to many people in their businesses and lives in general. I think it's time for me to have a mentor in my life and I'd like that to be you."

He looked at me quizzically and replied, "I'm not sure how I would be helpful in the line of business you are in now."

I smiled coyly, "I didn't say I was looking for a business mentor. You were suggesting last week that I should be able to ask for what I would like in bed, and I was hoping you could help me with that."

Now caressing my arm, The Mentor replied, "This is certainly not how I expected this evening to go."

His hotel room was luxurious, and I took a moment to appreciate my new surroundings for the night. And then it hit me ... Shit! I hadn't really thought so far ahead as to what might happen. I hadn't come prepared with non-latex condoms (since I am allergic to latex) and of course his condoms were latex. Not a problem. The Mentor wasn't fussed; he simply put his clothes back on to head to the store down the street. I sat back in the most comfortable bed in the world and anticipated what was coming next. The sex was excellent, but his mentoring skills were a bit lacking. Lust took over and we just did what came naturally; there wasn't actually any talking about what I liked. Which was quite okay with me because I was enjoying everything we were doing and preferred to just enjoy and not talk about it.

The next morning at breakfast in the fancy hotel dining room, The Mentor picked up his game. "That was well and good for the first time, but next time I am only going to take direction from you; you will need to tell me what you like." Joy and terror all wrapped into one little sentence. I spent the next week mentally preparing. Our text messages were more to plan our next rendezvous than anything else. I had been hopeful The Mentor would slip into a little sexting to help me get comfortable for our in-person session, but nope, that didn't happen.

I invited The Mentor to dinner, figuring he might appreciate a home-cooked meal as he spent so much time on the road. He did and we spent plenty of time eating and talking about things that never included what I might like in bed. I figured when we moved to the bedroom that would change, but again, it didn't – this was just like any other experience I had had. I enjoyed what we were doing and didn't feel the need to provide direction, and he didn't give any nor did he ask for any. It seemed his sexual skills far surpassed his mentoring skills.

This continued a while longer. Sometimes we would just meet for a meal and nothing more, sometimes we would meet for a meal and more, but the mentoring never really happened. And slowly he backed away. Given our previous conversations, I figured if he thought the sex was bad he'd be direct about that, although from my point of view, while it was great the first time we were together, what ended up being the last time was just alright. I was again left wondering what had happened. We'd had such a nice connection … Did he realize he was letting me down as a mentor? Was he actually cheating on his wife and feeling guilty? I may not have learned to ask for what I wanted in bed under his tutelage, but it seemed I had finally learned to ask "What is wrong with this situation?" rather than "What is wrong with me?" If I had to choose between the two lessons, I'd pick the one I learned.

CHAPTER FIFTEEN

Two steps back, two steps forward

WITH ALL THAT SELF-AWARENESS, I TRULY THOUGHT I WAS LEARNING and growing and *ready*. I had a few relationships under my belt, a few experiences that had lasted only a month or two, and way too many meet and greets and dead-end communications. I was feeling like I had seen it all, or at least enough, and experienced all the possibilities. I'd gotten to a place where I felt more confident in my ability to show up for myself and for someone else. I also felt confident in my ability to be vulnerable enough to allow someone in in a way where I gave of myself and gave them room to step up and reciprocate. I was also confident the universe would again put on my path the right man to continue to use my new skills and explore the things I still needed to experience. But I didn't want to force it; I'd learned to slow down the amount I was dating and trust a relationship would happen when it was meant to happen.

The Illusionist

Poof, there appeared out of nowhere a match with a man I didn't remember swiping right on. Looking at his profile and thinking I must have swiped right by mistake, I pondered what to do next. Before I could decide, he messaged suggesting a drink that evening next door to where I was working. Okay, he was making this easy – why not?

I found The Illusionist standing out front finishing a cigarette. I definitely would have swiped left if I'd known that. He was dressed impeccably, but not my taste, and he wasn't bad looking, but also not my taste. Fortunately, we both had time for just one drink so I wouldn't be wasting too much time. He apparently wasn't one to waste time in general – his wife had moved out only a week before and he'd be seeing her after our drink because he was going to see his kids for cake to celebrate his birthday. The drink with me was his birthday gift for himself. Good for him, but I was not interested in a smoker who was so recently out of his marriage. This wouldn't go anywhere.

As we continued talking while sipping our drinks, it became clear The Illusionist was also smart, well-read, well-traveled, had a good job, played guitar and wrote music, and was a little bitter about the marriage – but given the point in time, not overly so. I was beginning to find more likes than flaws and he was apparently smitten enough to ask for a date.

The date started strong ... a lovely restaurant with yummy food, a charming companion, a walk in the park and a kiss. Ugh. The kiss was awkward and not so good. Just when The Illusionist was beginning to grow on me, a bad kiss with no chemistry. I've been told if the kiss isn't good, the sex will be worse – I've never stuck around to find out if that is true.

But The Illusionist was extremely smart and witty and worked his charms to get me to see him again. The kiss was better that time – perhaps it was just nerves before? More well-planned (by him) dates ensued, along with fun, open communication, and then an invitation to his place for dinner. There is nothing sexier than a man with a beautiful home, standing in a well-equipped kitchen with the sleeves on his dress shirt rolled up, cooking a delicious dinner. Wow. Who would have guessed I'd be enjoying myself so immensely with this man? Yet, *I'd been learning*, so I wanted to take it a bit slow. I didn't want sex to cloud my judgment. So, after a delicious dinner, I resisted temptation; no clothes were stripped off, we made a plan for another date and I went home.

I was feeling good about how clearly I'd articulated my boundaries and intentions with The Illusionist. I'd had enough time playing around. The clothes would only come off if we decided to move this forward. He told me he agreed and it was worth the wait. Our communication about what was going on between us felt solid, and he started sharing his worry that perhaps it was too soon for him to be getting involved. The first drink was a lark – he didn't expect to meet someone who would be more than just something casual. I knew this, I'd been there before, which is why I'd made it a practice not to date men who'd just come out of relationships. So, while I wasn't surprised, I felt sad.

The Illusionist liked me, though, and didn't necessarily want to end things. He was at a crossroads. So I stepped in with a suggestion. "I've obviously been doing this a lot longer than you have and I feel like the connection we are developing is special and rare. The way I see it, you've got two choices. You can walk away and settle into single life and date around and come to realize how good this was then check back and see if I am still available, or we can continue on and I'll give you the space you need to find yourself while we continue to get to know each other." Not surprisingly, The Illusionist wasn't ready to make a decision. We decided to leave it at that for the time being. Fair enough. I'd learned, I'd grown, I knew what I wanted and I also knew there was no need to pressure him. I did ask only that if he decided to step away, he'd be up-front about that right away and wouldn't let it linger or just start seeing other women. He readily agreed.

Things continued to develop, and we planned our first weekend away. I was packed and ready and just waiting for word that The Illusionist had landed back from his business trip and was on his way to pick me up. My phone pinged: "I was up at 3 am and am too tired, I'm going to head home and sleep." I was disappointed, but of course I understood, so I simply replied saying, "Sleep well, what time should I expect you in the morning?"

Little did I know that was the last I would hear from The Illusionist.

My text message and phone call in the morning both went unanswered. I felt a sinking feeling in the pit of my stomach. I waited impatiently all day, but still no reply. The next day, I sent a text: "Can you please just text me that you are okay?" And poof, just as quickly as The Illusionist had appeared, he completely disappeared. No reply. After a few months of dating, with what I had thought had been *open and honest* communication, I was ghosted.

I was devastated. I buried myself in my work to try to stamp out the heartache. It didn't seem to be going away. I sent a long email to The Illusionist letting him know how hurt I was and asking why he couldn't be kind enough to just respond – after all, he had a daughter and I couldn't imagine he'd ever want her to be treated that way.

No reply.

I had done everything right. I was up-front with my communication, I valued us both equally in the relationship, and yet this terrible thing happened and I was having a hard time getting past it. I agonized over what had happened for months. *Why did he do this? What is wrong with me? What is wrong with him? How could he do this?* On the one hand, I had seen great potential in a relationship with this amazing man. On the other, I couldn't fathom how this same wonderful person I saw could be so horrible and cruel. Sadly, this felt familiar – had I actually learned anything since my divorce?

This cut me to the core. I was feeling like I'd learned so much, I'd felt so strong and confident in myself and my choices. Then my newfound beliefs were snapped away from me so quickly with this injustice that I couldn't begin to comprehend. How was I going to trust any man after this? How was I going to trust myself and my ability to make good choices in matters of the heart? What had I done wrong? I was fairly certain this had nothing to do with me and everything to do with him, but that didn't make any of it better. His actions scarred me. How long would it take before I'd be able to meet a new man and not wonder, *Will this happen again? Is he going to ghost me?* I wanted so badly to let go and to trust again, but that's easier said than done. Any lingering trust issues I may have had before this happened had been greatly magnified.

The reappearing act

It was months before I stopped feeling haunted by his disappearance on a daily basis, and more before I finally stopped thinking of The Illusionist and started dating again. Things were changing in my life; I decided to leave my job and start my own business. As I was walking home after signing the last of the paperwork freeing myself from my job, I started thinking about closure and how serendipitous it would be to see The Illusionist and get closure from him too. What's that saying ... be careful what you wish for?

I was walking home from work for the last time. The traffic light changed so I decided to walk straight ahead instead of turning left for my normal route. And there he was, walking towards me. The Illusionist had once again appeared out of nowhere. Seriously? Was it really possible I had just been thinking about this and now it was happening? Of all the people in the world, there was The Illusionist walking towards me and fixing his eyes on a point beyond me, clearly thinking I wouldn't stop him if I thought he didn't see me.

He was wrong. The Illusionist wasn't that lucky. Feeling bold, I stepped in front of him so there was no escape – he had to talk to me. After a minute of small talk, for an unknown reason The Illusionist felt the need to tell me he'd been finding there was an opportunity for a lot of good sex.

"It's good for you," I challenged him, "but how do you know they think it's good too?"

"They come back for more."

"Hmmm … That could just be because they are interested in trying to have a relationship with a successful man." That clearly stumped him, I could see it on his face. While he was pondering that, I asked, "So, what happened?"

"You're going there already?"

Already? It had been almost a year! What a fucker. And why would he think he should be talking to me about his sex life? How did I ever see anything positive in this man?

He finally spat out that he'd realized he wasn't ready for a relationship, and he couldn't quite find the words for why he couldn't have just told me that rather than ghosting me. Not a good answer but clearly The Illusionist wasn't the man I'd thought he was. Now I had my closure. Done.

Two steps back

Apparently, I wasn't smart enough yet to actually move on. The Illusionist suggested we grab a drink and I didn't just let it go. I wanted more of an answer about what had happened, and had a small hope that deep down he was actually a good guy and he just had some healing to do. We began messaging back and forth, just like old times. I sent him a text saying I was heading out to meet him. This time he didn't ghost me, but it wasn't much better. "I'm not going to be able to make it," was the only reply from The Illusionist.

No suggestion of why or an alternative plan. Would he have just left me sitting at a bar waiting if I hadn't sent that text? How stupid was I to go for this? I promised myself I would be smarter now. I didn't reply.

And then it happened … again … and again. I kept bumping into The Illusionist in different locations. The first two times I said hello while passing by; after that, I'd cross the street or walk away so he wouldn't see me. He also continued to pop up on the dating apps again and again. It was uncanny how frequently this happened. So much so that I finally swiped right. We matched instantly, which meant he had already swiped right on me. Then he messaged me immediately. I replied, "I can't help but wonder why the universe keeps throwing us together; perhaps we should meet for a coffee."

This time he showed up. It was uncomfortable. I didn't find him attractive and didn't enjoy his company. *This* was why the universe kept putting him in my pathway: so I could really get the closure I needed and deserved – confirmation there was absolutely nothing there. Thank you, universe! A good guy may be hiding out under there somewhere, but he wasn't going to surface any time soon. It was clear – I was done; I was over it. I was over him.

If only it were that easy. I saw The Illusionist another time or two and I ignored him. And then I was in a neighborhood I don't get to often, standing with a friend waiting for an Uber to pick us up. A car pulled up with a man and a woman in it. The Illusionist emerged to get money out of the ATM. I was so stunned to see him that without thinking I said hello and got into my Uber. "That was The Illusionist!"

I said to my friend, who was visiting from out of town and had been hearing about him since we had first met.

Only in my life does this sort of thing happen. After that terrible coffee 'date', I couldn't help but wonder why he still continued to show up? What did the universe want me to see or understand? He popped up again on a dating app. We matched. Once again, we flirted, the messages went on and on. Every day. We made plans to get together. The messages continued every day that week until the date. And then, of course, they stopped.

About a week later I got a message asking why I'd not been in contact. "Let me help you remember: you actually stopped the communication. We were messaging daily and made a plan to see each other. As per usual, you stopped contacting me that day rather than following though. I was genuine, clearly you are not. I am not interested in whatever game you are playing."

"So many assumptions," was his reply.

"If you say so. Please feel free to correct me," was my *finally* final message to The Illusionist.

I can't explain why I kept going back for more. The image of him in his kitchen making me dinner? The sweet letter from his son that he shared with me that brought him to tears? The rose-colored glasses that showed the good and hid the bad until it appeared yet again? I don't know, but that was it for me. After that, I swiped left when I saw The Illusionist on a dating app, but somehow his profile keeps coming back. Maybe it's the universe testing me to make sure I continue to swipe left and keep him out of my life.

The Widower

Finally putting The Illusionist out of my life for good seemed to have been just what I needed to really move forward. After a few dead-end meet and greets, I started chatting with a man who seemed promising. Scheduling a meet and greet was a bit of a challenge because he lived over an hour away and was the sole parent of four children since his wife had passed. The difficulty of scheduling ended up being a bonus as it gave us the opportunity to get to know each other a bit. The Widower would call and we'd easily talk for an hour. He also sent flirty text messages, poems and slightly erotic stories about us. It all felt very charming and romantic. But at the same time, for reasons I couldn't figure out, there was this 'or' in the back of my mind … *or*, I was being groomed.

$$\mathcal{S}$$

WAITING AT THE AGREED-UPON SPOT FOR THE WIDOWER TO ARRIVE, I started getting antsy as the meeting time approached and then passed. I tried to keep myself calm and occupied watching the people going by, noticing how they walked and deciding what kind of person they were based on that. In between that, I worried I had been stood up and willed myself not to text him because if he was just late, he would actually be driving and I should just be patient.

Twenty minutes later I saw a man approaching – it was The Widower. He had a nice walk. He looked different than his photos, but quite handsome. I smiled acknowledgement, he gave me a big hug and a kiss on the cheek and apologized for being late – he'd had a hard time finding parking. He was clearly a bit flustered by his tardiness but started to relax as we walked to find a restaurant. The Widower made a comment about his five children, to which I replied, "I thought you said you had four."

"That must have been a typo," he replied, and just for a second I thought to myself, *That's odd. I'm fairly certain he told me each of their names and ages in text, so that's a big typo.* But he was so nonchalant about it I let it go without another thought.

The restaurant we walked to was the nicest in the area and he seemed to know it well. He ordered a lovely bottle of champagne to get us started and made suggestions of items we could share on the menu, starting with a dozen oysters. This Widower had good taste. Delicious food, a beautiful restaurant and flowing conversation; it felt like a very special evening and more like a first date than a meet and greet. The Widower mentioned his wife and I asked if he minded sharing how she passed. I expected cancer would be his reply and hoped I didn't look horrified when he told me she'd committed suicide. Luckily, he found her before the children saw her. He told me they were all doing remarkably well given the circumstances. This had been three years ago.

The serious conversation eased back into lighter chitchat and we laughed and chatted until we realized the restaurant was closing down around us. My favorite type of date. He insisted on paying for dinner and wouldn't even let me pay for an Uber home – he hired one for me on his account. I was riding high all the way home and the following days as the flirty messages and calls continued. I felt like the luckiest girl alive and that I had quite possibly found a wonderful man.

On the morning of our next date, he messaged me to say he had to postpone because of something with the kids. I was disappointed but understood and asked if we could at least have a phone call. Something had me on edge. Was this a repercussion from The Illusionist's ghosting or something else? As we spoke, I was honest and up-front with him, sharing that while I understood his reasons, I also felt a bit anxious because of past experiences and I knew that was me, not him, but it played into trust issues I had. The Widower said he understood and did his best to put a smile back on my face. We rescheduled the date for a few nights later when he could get away. Why couldn't I shake this anxiety then? Was it remnants of past dating trauma or was it intuition?

Since I was now free for the evening, I turned on the TV and saw there was a brand-new series I'd never heard of on Netflix. Still feeling in a funk from the disappointment of the canceled date I had so been looking forward to, I didn't have the energy to search for something else, so I just watched that. It was good, it took my mind off everything and I continued to binge watch. Well past midnight, I was still watching but starting to get sleepy when a scene came on about a man lying about his wife being dead. That woke me up and put shivers through my body. It felt like I was meant to see this.

The Widower had given me his last name and shown me pictures of his kids – he couldn't have been hiding anything, right? It wouldn't hurt to do a simple search on his *dead* wife's name; surely I wouldn't find anything out of order. Yet there it was, staring me in the face a minute later as I was scanning her Facebook page, horrified. This woman who had been dead for three years had been posting pictures with their kids in the past few months. I felt sick to my stomach. I couldn't process this information and I couldn't call anyone to help – all of my friends were long asleep by now. I turned off the TV and tried to go to sleep but couldn't. I tossed and turned, with so many thoughts going through my mind that I didn't sleep a wink that night.

Two steps forward

By morning, I knew what I had to do: carry on with The Widower as if nothing had happened. He had no idea I knew, and I was also fairly certain that if he was lying about this, if I called him out on it he would just block me from contacting him. So, when he sent sweet, flirty text messages in the morning, I replied in kind, as I would have before knowing what I knew. That was hard; I've never been very good at hiding my feelings or patiently awaiting what was to come next.

I casually suggested we meet at a cool new bar for a drink before heading off to the dinner reservation he'd made for our next date. He agreed, having no idea I did that because I didn't want to be alone with him and we likely wouldn't make it to the dinner reservation. I brought a friend and her husband along to the bar for moral support and safety – I had no idea what else The Widower was capable of. They sat down the bar a bit and I nodded slightly to them as The Widower walked in. This man who I found so attractive and charming just a week ago now looked to me quite disheveled and unattractive and coarse. This time my skin crawled as he hugged and kissed me hello. Could this really be the same man? Had my perception of him on each date have so thoroughly altered what he looked like each time? Apparently, beauty *is* in the eye of the beholder.

We weren't there for long before The Widower asked if I was okay. I seemed a bit off to him. If only he knew! I asked how many children he *really* had, was it four or was it five? That no longer seemed like a typo – now it was an important detail that everything hinged on. The pictures I saw on Facebook had five redheads who were clearly siblings, but the youngest was under two, proving his wife couldn't have been dead for three years. I didn't let on that I knew that. Clearly, he figured I had some other information as he confessed that he actually had one more wife than he had previously told me about, for a total of three past wives and 11 children. I asked him to tell me about each and at the end informed him that once again his numbers didn't add up – that only made 10; there was one more. He realized his error with the youngest and said that he had also taken custody of one of his grandchildren who 'they' adopted, but he didn't want to talk about it.

I press on with The Widower – who is 'they'? He and the dead wife – who else? I asked how they could have adopted him if she died three years ago and he wasn't yet three? Maybe it wasn't three years ago, he told me, saying that information was between him and his *supposedly* dead wife and no one else. He wanted to know why I was pressing him on this. So I told him about the Facebook page, and he tried to explain it away.

"You know I don't believe in social media and I've heard before there are some strange pictures out there that make no sense." He wouldn't look at the pictures and insisted they were taken long ago – but they couldn't have been, because the pictures she posted were of the kids at the same age as the pictures he had shown me, not three years earlier. When I insisted it didn't add up, his reply was, "Why did you agree to see me, Julie, if this is what you wanted to do? Why did you bring me all the way here for this? You do realize that if there isn't trust, there is no point in a relationship, so I think I'd better just go."

Yes, obviously, The Widower was right – this was *my* fault for not trusting him. I don't know what his intention had been with all of this, but I'd gotten smarter, I had learned. I didn't let it fester or linger on, and I didn't let him ghost me. I made sure he was there to be held accountable, even though he wasn't man enough to own up to whatever it was he was doing. Not that I really expected he would. Before getting up to leave he said to me, "Is there anything you need before I go?"

In my head I replied, "Absolutely, you bastard, I need you to 'fess up, tell me the truth, go home to your wife and stop this nonsense." But I just sat there stone cold and watched him walk away.

I joined my friends down the bar. They wanted details immediately and I asked for their patience for a minute so I could report him on the app. His profile was gone; he had clearly walked out the door and deleted me, thinking I wouldn't be able to report him. This guy had done this before – he was a pro. But I was too. I'd taken pictures of his profile in case this happened, so I was still able to report him and provide his phone number too. They assured me The Widower would be banned forever.

While I considered it, I decided not to try to let The Widower's *not-so-dead* wife know what her husband was doing. I remembered that The Widower knew my address from sending me home in an Uber. Had that been another calculated move on his part in case anything like this ever happened so he would know I knew he knew where I lived? I had no idea what more this man was capable of, but I certainly wasn't going to take any chances, so I just let it go.

He did show up with the same profile on another app a year later and I reported him there too – they said they would remove him. I've since moved so he can't easily find me, but it scares me to think what this man could be capable of and how many women in addition to his wife he is turning into victims.

I took off my own rose-colored glasses and stood up to The Widower. I did that to stand up for myself. It felt like progress. It did still leave another scar on my memory and my heart, making it a bit more difficult to feel like I could trust. At least when I shared this story with others, they were sympathetic to the fact I had been treated badly. I read about a journalist who was seeing a man for about a year before she realized the man she was in love with was leading a double life. People weren't as kind to her. On top of the pain of what had been done to her, she had to live with her friends and family questioning why she hadn't discovered this sooner … after all, she was an investigative journalist – she should have known. Really? WTF is wrong with people? This woman was a victim who deserved their love and support, not their questioning of her intellect and ability. She had enough trauma, questioning herself and any future man in her life, without anyone else layering more of that on.

CHAPTER SIXTEEN

Is there really no other way?

I'VE HAD SO MANY EXPERIENCES THOUGH ONLINE DATING, SOME POS-
itive, others not so much. This mirrors the stories I've read about and
heard about firsthand, and from hundreds of others who have turned
to online dating looking for anything from a one-night stand to a last
first date for the rest of their lives. The commonality in what I've heard
is apathy.

"Are you using the dating apps?"

"Yes, only because there doesn't seem to be another way. I keep
getting tired and going off again and then I realize there is no other
option and try again."

While there are some who love the apps (mostly people who are
new to them or used them years ago and found their significant other),
there are so many more that have, *at best*, a love/hate relationship with
them. I feel the same.

I fear the apps have created in us a culture of apathy, not just
for the apps, but towards each other and forming real, meaningful

relationships. And this isn't just in my age group. I've spoken to singles from their early twenties to their late seventies who are all experiencing the same. It leaves me feeling sad … and still single. Yet the optimist in me believes my match is still out there and we will find each other at the right time.

Amidst the struggle and negativity, there are some truly lovely people on the apps. I have had lovely meet and greets and even first dates with men who I enjoyed meeting but were just not my Mr Forever. I've learned new things from some of these men and appreciated the time we spent together, even if we just weren't intended to stay in each other's lives. I hope they feel the same way about having met me.

Some matches also resulted in very generous offers of support from men who were practically strangers – men I'd conversed with but hadn't yet met. One guy offered me a place to stay for two nights when I was in need, another offered to hang my artwork, another to provide free assessment services for storm damage on my home, and there are other kind offers and deeds I could add to that list. I am grateful for those offers, some of which I even accepted. Those men helped me overcome my fear of appearing weak by accepting help and taught me an even bigger lesson that I could accept help without feeling like I needed to offer anything in exchange outside of thanks and appreciation. None of them ever made me feel indebted to them in any way or asked for anything in return. I've always been much better at the giving end of these equations than the receiving side, so these experiences were huge lessons that were a testament to my growth in understanding my own value and the good nature of so very many people.

While I saw the beautiful side of people and that gives me hope, I've also found online dating perpetuates a litany of bad behavior which saddens me to no end. Rather than gloss over or ignore this behavior, I believe it's important to bring it the forefront of our attention and talk about it, so we are all aware it exists. That way we can recognize it if it is happening to us, call it out for what it is and, most importantly, move forward to change it rather than simply ignore it.

Fakes

I can spot the majority of fake profiles a mile away, so why can't the apps figure it out and delete them? "I am a God-fearing man working on an offshore oil rig or in gemstones currently stationed in some Middle Eastern country" and similar-type language is usually a sign the profile is a fake. These fake profiles are often also widowers with children living with another relative while they are off working. They sometimes say they are from where you live and will be returning soon. Their pictures are attractive, but if you look closely, you will realize they look more like stock photo images or that they have been photoshopped ... it's often subtle enough to miss. If you ask too many questions or start pushing too much for specifics, they will usually delete you. Sometimes immediately, other times overnight, likely thinking it won't be as obvious they have disappeared.

While there are many reasons for fake profiles, none of which are any good, they are usually set up to scam you. Keep yourself safe from these people. Please do not give away too much personal information! Don't give out any personally identifiable information like your last name, birthday, home address or email. If someone immediately asks you to switch to email or Skype or some other identifying platform before you've actually met them, please beware and don't do it! Better safe than sorry. I do always exchange mobile numbers before actually meeting someone so I know they are real and that if something were to happen, someone could track them though my phone records.

In the early days, I amused myself by playing along with a few of the fake accounts to see what would happen. I've heard stories of others who have done the same. I was actually 'engaged' to one of them, at least in his fake account mind. I played along for a while but just couldn't bring myself to tell him how much I loved him and missed him and couldn't wait until we could finally be together and get married, so it fizzled. Another was on a peace-keeping mission in some far-off land and wanted to leave early to come be with me, but needed money to get the plane ticket because, since he was taking early leave, his employer was withholding his pay. We even had phone conversations, which surprised me, but I guess they need to do that to get you to believe they are real. He gave me instructions on where to wire the money and I pretended that my bank couldn't wire it to a Western Union and would need his bank details instead. I thought maybe I could catch him that way. When that didn't work, I told him I had bad news: that I had seen one of my good friends, who was an FBI agent, and he was worried this guy was a fake and wouldn't let me wire the money until I provided the address of the house his daughter lived in. He got very upset, asking how I couldn't trust him when he loved me so much, and then called me incessantly to the point where

I even wondered if he was real and not a scam. He finally stopped calling and I decided to stop wasting my time trying to catch these guys. At the time, I found it mildly amusing and thought I was doing a service to other women trying to catch them. But they are pros – they won't let you catch them, and they will do everything they can to get you to second-guess yourself and think, *Maybe they are actually real, or they wouldn't go on and on like this.* The romantic in me wanted to think it was possible that a guy could be saying all the right things and be real ... it *could* be possible, just not with these guys!

Bottom line: stay away from fake profiles and report them.

Liars

Lies show up in online dating in so many ways, shapes and forms. It feels like the apps intrinsically encourage rather than discourage lying. Let's start with the small lies: old pictures in the profile, or professing to be taller, shorter, wider, thinner, older, younger than the profile says. Someone lists interests that they aren't really interested in or they omit information that would be important to share ... like that they are actually married. Some of those are seemingly small enough lies, but why do they happen so often? Do the liars think someone will get to know them and like them so much they won't mind? Are they secretly thinking, *Once I get in front of you, I will be so charming and irresistible that nothing else will matter?*

Lies of omission get more serious if they have to do with relationship status or what a person says they are looking for in a match. For example, a man just wants sex but says he is interested in dating, or omits that he is married from his profile, but then reveals he is married, or, worse yet, continues to infer he is single. I use the pronoun 'he' because my experience is with dating men, but I have heard stories from men that some women's profiles have these lies too. Is going into a relationship with any kind of lie a good way to start? Or is it so commonplace no one seems to care? Or doesn't it even matter anymore? An even bigger question is, why do people spend so much time lying on the dating apps? What is the actual benefit? Once someone gets comfortable lying on dating apps with no consequences or repercussions, do they then start feeling comfortable lying in other areas of their lives?

The most egregious thing about the liars is they don't take into consideration anyone but themselves. The world revolves round them and their lies and they don't seem to notice or care if there is collateral damage.

Double standards

The double standards irk me to no end. For example, it's okay for him to cheat, that isn't a problem, but it's not okay for me to tell his wife – that would just be wrong. Of course, I am so sorry I would have even mentioned it. WTF? Yes, this really happens; here's a real-life example word for word:

Him (after a week of messages back and forth suggesting he was single): "Actually, I'm married. But don't worry, it's not a problem."

Me: "Oh, so you are in an open relationship?"

"No, but she's in a different state right now."

"I'm going to take a pass, I don't want to get into a situation where a spouse could get hurt."

"Oh, she won't get hurt. She's in another state."

"So if I contacted her and said I've been speaking with you here, she wouldn't be hurt by that?"

"Why would you do that? What kind of awful person are you? If you would do something like that, I wouldn't want to be associated with you."

"I've simply pointed out that you are married and your wife could get hurt by this, I don't even have a way to contact her, I was just making a point."

"You are truly a nasty woman."

And with that he deleted me. Yes, he's cheating on his wife, I want nothing to do with it, and *I* am the bad person. True story.

These double standards can come from men or women, I am just on the end of experiencing them from men because that is who I date. Men who think it's okay for them to be doing a myriad of things that the woman they are looking to date should or shouldn't do: date other people, be willing to date someone who is married, be available on demand, have certain traits they don't themselves have ... and the list goes on.

There seems to be a double standard surrounding age, too. I've never heard of a younger woman saying to an older man, "Are you okay with going out with someone younger?" But I've heard that many times from younger men. We've both set age limits on our profiles and they state our ages, so why is that question even necessary? It feels like a subtle power play or way of saying, without specifically stating, "I just want to remind you I am younger and you should be grateful I am interested in you."

In dating – and life in general, really – we'd be so much better off if we didn't have different standards for others than we do for ourselves. A good way to put this into action is to check yourself, and if there is a standard you want to hold others to, make sure it's something you offer yourself – and if it isn't, work on yourself before expecting others to meet that standard.

Love bombing

Someone comes in hard and fast. They are extremely attentive and want to spend a lot of time together and quickly lead you to believe they are The One. This is love bombing. Of course, this happened before online dating too, but it seems to have proliferated with online dating. The hard thing with love bombing, at least for me, is the romantic in me wants to believe that there is a chance this isn't actually love bombing – this is real! This guy is The One and we are going to live happily ever after. Unfortunately, that's not the case the majority of the time and as hard and fast as they come in, the gaslighting, ghosting or other abusive behavior starts to follow. The trick here is to be able to decipher this behavior and run as fast as you can in the other direction. A good way to be able to detect and avoid it is to start out slow.

I experienced this with a guy who I dated for a few months. He kept pushing me to see him more often and showered me with gifts and made me feel special. When I finally stepped into it and agreed to enter a relationship, he decided overnight that we were through because he wasn't over the ex-girlfriend who he had been telling me was so awful for him and ruined his life. I later learned this was a pattern for him. If you get caught in this trap, remember it's them, it's not you; please don't let them make you feel badly about yourself when they withdraw their attention, or let them leave you feeling it was something you did wrong. Let them go; you deserve better.

Ghosting

The original definition of ghosting was "the appearance of a ghost or secondary image on a television or other display screen" but no one remembers that because now ghosting is so commonplace and readily accepted behavior that a new definition has been added to the dictionary: "the practice of ending a personal relationship with someone by suddenly and without explanation withdrawing from all communication".

I don't think I have spoken to a single person who hasn't been ghosted by someone on a dating app at some point in time. It is now, seemingly and sadly, a readily accepted way to end a relationship or any kind of communication at all. I've had it all happen to me way too many times and in more ways than with The Illusionist – but never as deep into a relationship as I was with him. It can be as simple as matching with someone I am excited to match with, and then the match disappears. Or more involved: I send a message or reply to a message and then no word; I start a conversation with someone and sometimes even mid-sentence, the match disappears; I set up a meet and greet with someone I've been messaging with multiple times and then, the day of the meet and greet, no word and no meeting. I even sent a message to one saying, "Hey, are you okay – or do you just think it's okay to set a date and then stop communicating, and if you think it's okay, can you let me know how you figure that?" No response, unless you call deleting me a response.

Is it ghosting if you match, don't have any communication and then they delete the match? The answer to that question shouldn't matter; it shouldn't be happening. But it *is* happening and for a number of reasons, some of which I would imagine I don't even know about. One reason it happens (so I've been told by multiple men) is that they just swipe right on women to improve their odds and then when they match they decide if they are interested, and if they aren't, hit delete. How and why have these sorts of things become acceptable behavior? They shouldn't be. But so many people I've spoken to take it in stride as if it is actually a feature of dating apps. They say it doesn't bother them, but statistics on dating app usage and correlating depression and anxiety rates would say otherwise. At what point does or should common courtesy play into this? And why are we so ready to accept and ignore bad behavior? And what can we do about it anyhow? If someone isn't responding because they have ghosted you, there is no way to get a message across to call them out on it.

If you go on a meet and greet and no one follows up from there, is that acceptable and does it mean no one has been ghosted? I'd venture to say yes but I do wish there was a better way to get some clarity here in case one person is hoping or waiting to hear from the other. Kindness and closure would be so much better for everyone's mental health. Maybe we need to start teaching people how to have these conversations so that it becomes second nature and easier than ghosting?

Why?

Why have we, as a human race, allowed all of this to become acceptable behavior? Why do these things happen? Hard to say for sure, but I think there are a few reasons.

Bad actors: There are just some bad people out there who are self-serving and don't think how their actions – often bad actions – will impact others. They simply don't care. The only way they will stop their behavior is for the good actors to send them packing. So please, if you come across these types, walk away and don't reward them with your attention. Don't let them step into or stomp on your life. Hold them accountable for their behavior.

Lost souls: People who really don't know who they are or what they want and often don't know how to communicate, so they end up misleading others as they stumble through figuring out who they are or what they want. The good news is, these people can take action and figure out who they are and what they want.

Fear and insecurity: People who are scared of putting themselves out there and scared of getting hurt. They have similar behavior to the lost souls and may add in a bit of passive-aggressive behavior tied to letting their pride get in the way of expressing themselves openly and authentically.

False expectations: The way the dating apps have been set up and have evolved gives us the belief that there is a never-ending supply of potential matches. So we set our expectations too high on what each match should bring, and therefore falsely believe there will be someone better than the person in front of us coming along. We also falsely believe we should have a connection with each of the people we meet, and when that doesn't happen, we get jaded and start thinking the process isn't working.

SO WHERE TO FROM HERE? IT FEELS LIKE SOMETHING HAS TO CHANGE. It feels like the dating apps are playing into our worst human characteristics. And the statistics out there would say that is true, because people on dating apps are experiencing *more* loneliness, anxiety and depression rather than *less*. This feels very broken.

CHAPTER SEVENTEEN

Looking to the future

WHAT DOES ALL OF THIS MEAN? WHERE DO I GO FROM HERE? WHERE do we all go from here?

It doesn't seem like the dating apps are going away – statistically, they are the main way people are meeting. Maybe we will just need to start being better versions of ourselves so we can make the most of them. I'm about to share a recipe for success here, yet I am still single! I get the irony in that. Yet, while I am still single and have my own love/hate relationship with dating apps, I 100 percent believe I will find the right partner and right relationship for me. It might be using one of the apps; it might not. I am an optimist, after all, so I am doing my best to stay open to the possibilities.

We can be better than this

I believe we have an opportunity to be, and *can* be, better versions of ourselves. For ourselves, and for each other. Let's stop with all those bad behaviors and be kind to each other on dating apps … and in real life, too. I know I would much rather put myself out there in a real and authentic way and try to connect with someone rather than just thinking it isn't possible and not trying. It doesn't mean it will be easy, it doesn't mean I won't come up against some bad actors or get hurt, but if I show up in that way, I have a much better chance of finding the partner I would like to have.

If we all do that, if we all show up and are open and honest, there is a larger pool of great people to date. So let's do this together, shall we? As much as this is an individual journey and we each need to find our own way, I have a few suggestions that can serve as positive guidelines:

- **Work on yourself:** Get clear on who you are, what you want, how you want to show up and who and what you are looking for.

- **Be honest and clear:** Have an honest profile and clearly articulate who you are and what you want.

- **Be open:** Put yourself out there in an open and authentic manner, even if that means you can get hurt. You also have more opportunity to experience love and joy!

- **Give people a chance:** Limit your deal-breakers and be really open to meeting someone – and don't be too quick to discount them thinking there are 100 more options.

- **Be kind to others**: Treat others with respect. Don't ghost – follow through. And if you aren't interested, let them down gently – don't let them linger.

- **Be kind to yourself:** If someone isn't treating you with the respect you deserve, realize it's them, not you, and move on. Take a break from dating if you are feeling apathetic or over it; you can always come back later.

- **Enjoy the journey:** Remember to keep it positive and enjoyable – have fun with it.

- **Take your time:** Patience can be hard, but don't artificially rush things along.

- **Shift your mindset about meet and greets:** Before dating apps, I'd go out to a party or a bar and talk to 10 different guys or more. If I didn't click with one, the conversation would end. If I take that forward to today, that should be how I think about a meet and greet. But I've been placing much higher expectations on each meet and greet because the effort is similar to what in that pre-app world was a date. I'm realizing I need to shift my expectations to know it is okay, and normal, to have a number of meet and greets that just end there and I need to be fine with that.

Somewhere along the way, I found myself

Wow! What a journey this has been. While I know there is always more to learn, I feel good about where I am now. I've found myself, mostly. And in doing that, I've learned so much about what I want for myself, for my life, and what I want in a partner. I now feel like I am ready to meet *him*. There were times I thought I was ready before, but maybe I wasn't.

There were a lot of things I needed to *un*learn along the way. A lot of *shoulds* ... who I *should* be, who I *should* be with, what that relationship *should* be like, how/when/why sex *should* figure into that relationship. I've explored my boundaries, pushed my boundaries, taken myself outside of my comfort zone and come to a place where I love, appreciate and respect myself – so it is now more available to me to be able to love, appreciate and respect my future partner when we find each other.

I used to crave a relationship and it continued to elude me. And then, over time, I came to realize the relationship I was craving so badly was with myself. Once I found that, I let go of the need for someone else to love me. Now it is simply something I desire to have in my life, and I feel better equipped to recognize that man when we meet and step into a healthy, positive relationship with him. I've let go of that attachment to wanting to be liked by every man I go on a date with and am doing my best to remain unattached to outcomes so that it can just unfold and happen as it is intended to.

I'm excited for my future relationship; I trust that it will come when the time is right and that I am much better prepared to enjoy the journey to get there. I wish the same for you.

Epilogue

Sitting on my bed in a fully furnished apartment, physically and emotionally a world away from where I started, I chuckle to myself, realizing here I am again with pen and paper – this time editing rather than writing. So much has transpired, so much has been learned, and at the same time so much is the same. Another day, another interaction with a man I met on Tinder that has left me baffled and a bit ticked off. But tonight I won't lose any sleep over it; tonight I will sleep well because I can easily let it go, knowing, really knowing, I deserve better and I will find better. Tonight, I go to sleep by myself knowing one night there will be an amazing man lying here with me in this bed. Now that I've found myself and value myself, we can find each other in the right way, when the time is right, and it will be magical. Until then, I'm quite happy and content. Knowing this and feeling this to the core of my being, the tears I have been holding back for so long finally come; they are tears of happiness. It's been a lot of work and discovery and a long time coming to feel like this.

EVEN WITH ALL THAT I HAVE LEARNED, IN MANY RESPECTS I STILL have more questions than answers. I believe there is a better way. I continue to ponder what that is. I would love nothing more than to make that happen, for me, for you and the rest of the world. Our happiness depends on it. I believe in collective wisdom, that alone I can have some impact, and together we can do more.

If you would like to keep up with what I have planned or submit your own dating story or a suggestion on the best path forward, please go to www.founddating.com. I would love to hear from you. Let's work together to find true love and make this world a better place for us all.

Thanks for sharing my journey, and 1 look forward to creating the next chapter with and for you.

xo,

Julie

Bonus:
Just for giggles

There are so many other little quips and experiences and *are you kidding me is this for real* moments that were just so funny and sometimes unbelievable. So sit back and have a laugh, let your jaw drop when you can't believe these things actually happened, and enjoy … oh, and if you have a story you'd like to share, please visit: www.founddating.com and submit it!

Just when I was having a day where I was feeling completely over all this online dating, a message came in from a really hot guy saying, "I know you've been told you have a nice … but I just had to tell you that I think you are BEAUTIFUL!"

How could that not make a girl's day? Funny how I could let one little message like that change my perspective on how I was feeling about online dating, and life in general too.

"I'm going out on a limb here (in answer to your question about what people first notice …) and say, one: your smoldering eyes! Two, your beautiful skin! And there, wait, is this being recorded? No? Ok. Then, your boobies! There, I said it … and probably disqualified myself, or have you writing down my info … promise you won't be disappointed! Usually I channel my southern roots to describe myself but you seem to bring out a different side. I am, and will be a good guy to you, it's just an instinctive reaction … and really think it's in your eyes. Must be a Scorpio. Let me know if I'm still within bounds, and if so, what it will take to meet you in person."

Boobies? This guy is over 50 – there should be a law that you can't use that word if you are over 10! I didn't reply straight away and then got a message from him apologizing for speaking to me in such a fresh manner and getting carried away and not being a gentleman. I replied, "apology accepted", and he wrote back that I was very kind and to hold out for a good guy. Maybe he was a good guy and I missed out? Or maybe not.

ℒ

Another one in response to my "I've been told I have a nice …" line was the reply: "I've been told I have a huge …" Now that one got my attention. Okay, get your mind out of the gutter! Because he was funny, not because he has something huge, although that might not have been a bad thing, I suppose ;-).

ℒ

"I'm sure you are told that you have a very inviting smile, it caught my attention. A few questions for you ... do you think you can get a crush on someone via e-mail? Has your taste in men changed over the years? And what do you think of this match thing? Ciao Bella."

How does one respond to that? I couldn't figure it out either, so he didn't get a response ☹.

ℒ

"Hi beautiful, just wanted to let you know that I'm still interested, hope to hear from you, you're a hottie" ... I replied to this message and then I never heard from him again.

ℒ

"I like your style and your swagger. You have a great smile. You are beautiful! You're really cute, adorable."

That was in the first message, the second message came before I could respond.

"Hi again, I want to meet you. You have a really beautiful face. Would love to share a passionate kiss."

Very sweet, but do I want to be talking about passionate kisses with a stranger? There were quite a few steps missing to get to the point where I would consider that, but then, I guess they wouldn't be a stranger at that point.

ℒ

"Good morning! You do look like you are from somewhere else! No idea? I like the look! I'd love to meet for coffee if you are up for it! ..."

I wrote back, "I don't think that's a good idea."

That's it, that's all I said.

Harsh, you say? Wait, don't be so quick to criticize – this was an ex-ROOMMATE who had a big crush on me and had actually once asked me, "If you weren't my roommate would you be interested in dating me?" This was the same roommate I later learned was overcharging me for rent, so I moved out. Interesting choice of how to get back in touch, no? Still think that reply was too harsh?

⍋

Scene: First date after solid meet and greet.

Me: "Wait, so for the six years you've been here, you are actually still married, your child is back in Italy with your wife and she isn't an ex-wife? I don't date married men."

Him (said with strong Italian accent): "No, no but it's okay, she no here and I no ask you to marry me, so it no problem."

And there you have it, he won't be asking me to marry him, so it's all okay. Interesting how my wants or needs didn't even figure in there.

Acknowledgements

YOU'VE HEARD THE SAYING: 'IT TAKES A VILLAGE TO RAISE A CHILD'? I've always adapted that to say: 'It takes a village to raise an adult'. And now I will extend that to: 'It takes a village to publish a book'! So I want to thank my village for helping me to be the adult and author that I have become. First, I need to start with you, my readers – you inspired me to write this book and I thank you for reading it. I sincerely hope that it has an impact on you and those in your current and future villages.

I need to extend my thanks to the characters in the book … those who will recognize themselves in it, and those who may not or might not ever know they are in it. The ones who do, you are so very special to me and have had a profound impact on my life and ability to write this book. And the ones who don't you have helped me to learn some important lessons that have deeply impacted me and the content of this book.

I have close friends on multiple continents who are my chosen family and as much as I would like to name you all here, because there are no names in the book, I will be thanking you each individually in a less public forum. You each have helped to make me a better person and to want to be a better person and I thank you all for the laughs, love, support, community and magic ... oh the magic ... may it be contagious. And to my birth family, your support and encouragement has also allowed me to soar and follow my dreams – I love you.

To K & L – wow I couldn't have done this without your talent – you are an amazing team who have taken this book to a whole new level it wouldn't have reached without you.

And to the man that I've yet to meet ... This is a love letter to you and to me and to all that we will be.

xo,
Julie

About the Author

Julie Demsey is a recovered tech executive and sought after transformational mindset coach and hypnotherapist, helping her clients to break through blocks and limiting beliefs to reach their full potential personally and professionally.

She believes it is necessary to be kinder to ourselves so we can be kinder to others and create the lives we desire.

For more on Julie visit **www.juliedemsey.com** and **www.founddating.com**

Made in the USA
Las Vegas, NV
11 February 2021